I0115935

The Job

of

Environmental Protection

A Field Guide to
Policy Implementation

Peter Pagano

Arrowsic Island Press

Copyright © 2010 Peter Pagano
All rights reserved.

ISBN: 061534352X
ISBN-13: 9780615343525
Library of Congress Control Number: 2009914017

Arrowsic Island Press
Bethesda, Maryland

Contact us by email: arrowsicpress@gmail.com

To Isabella, Rose, Grace

and

Moira

CONTENTS

PREFACE

The premise of this book is well summarized by Wallace Stegner who wrote "Environmentalism or conservation or preservation, or whatever it should be called, is not a fact, and never has been. It is a job."[1] To protect the environment, or mitigate adverse impacts in order to preserve biodiversity, you have to put regulatory programs into practice. Like many jobs, there are many obstacles and challenging tasks that require the long term commitment of effort and resources in order to achieve measureable success.

This book presents first person accounts of fieldwork implementing state land use laws in order to illustrate the practical considerations for policy makers and citizens to be aware of as they move forward to address environmental issues. The first chapters provide background on environmental law enforcement as a policy tool and describe the typical roles and responsibilities of the person in the field. Subsequent chapters begin with a discussion of basic ecology and a cursory summary of the pertinent regulatory requirements only in so much as to provide an introductory context for the principles, intricacies and practical reality of what it takes to direct human behavior to preserve the environment through policy implementation. A broad spectrum of activities effecting several types of ecologically sensitive areas are illustrated.

The examples are presented so that elements of implementation common to any environmental law are highlighted. The elements are presented in a law enforcement context including: conducting an investigation, gathering evidence, managing a caseload, calculating penalties, drafting and negotiating settlements, balancing enforcement discretion with voluntary compliance, as well as working with agencies, the media, and the general public. In addition, ethical and political issues associated with the decision-making for these elements will be discussed. In presenting these elements, I have also attempted to convey the time frame associated with various activities to demonstrate the complexity of achieving various milestones.

The cases utilized here were selected primarily for illustrative purposes. The lessons that can be drawn from them can be extrapolated to far more complex regulatory requirements and cases that involve far greater economic impacts (i.e. hazardous waste disposal, oil spills, air and water emissions, etc.). In summary, the book utilizes simple examples to illustrate the basic tasks and concepts for effectively implementing environmental programs. These tasks and concepts are common to the implementation of any environmental program, whether it's designed to save a stream or mitigate climate change.

CHAPTER I

THE RULE OF LAW

Laws set standards for our society. Environmental laws are intended to protect natural resources and to prevent pollution. An environmental law – or any law for that matter – is not worth the paper it is written on if it is not enforced. Enforcement of the law is not an end in itself, but is the necessary policy implementation activity to create rational incentives for people to comply with the common will. Enforcement powers are not self-implementing; whether they provide a powerful tool for achieving policy goals requires government agencies to be proactive in their implementation. State and federal environmental agencies have enforcement programs to make sure that the laws get the results that the public wants.

The fundamental goal of enforcement is to convince those who are regulated that it is better to comply than to wait until they are caught and subjected to an enforcement action. An enforcement action is a response to something a person or company has done in violation of a law or regulation. Every violation requires a response. The type of response will typically be in keeping with the seriousness of the violation. It can range from informal actions that take little effort; to formal ones involving a large commitment of resources and the assessment of fines. In choosing the most appropriate response, a regulatory agency will attempt to achieve several goals: correction of the violation as soon as possible; effective use of resources by using the action that achieves the greatest environmental benefit; punishment of serious, willful wrongdoing;

fairness to the regulated community by treating similar violations in a like manner; and the deterrence of future violations.

The motivation for an entity to comply with environmental laws is influenced by several incentives and disincentives. Incentives that favor compliance include: societal or moral factors, such as the fundamental sense of social responsibility to obey the laws of the land, and the belief that protection of the environment is a civic and personal duty. The economic advantages of compliance can potentially include reduced materials and/or waste disposal costs as a result of recycling, or the marketing of an environmentally friendly (i.e. green) image. Disincentives that may work against compliance include: The concern for individual property rights, which leads some people to view environmental regulations as an intrusion on their right to conduct their business as they see fit, including the economic advantage gained by not investing money for compliance.

Regulatory agencies intervene in the conflict between incentives and disincentives with their enforcement activities, adding new motivating forces to tip the scales in favor of compliance. Two broad strategies are used: 1. Compliance Promotion/Assistance: The regulatory agency makes systematic efforts to lead people to voluntarily comply with the law. For example, outreach efforts that provide training and technical assistance to the regulated community on a law's requirements and how they can be met; 2. Enforcement Actions: Specific responses to violations in which a regulatory agency seeks to compel a particular entity to comply.

Environmental regulatory agencies create and maintain a credible enforcement presence by conducting inspections which generate the perception that there is a likelihood of detection. To maintain the presence, once a violation is detected, it must also lead to serious consequences such as penalties. Penalties are not just a source of revenue for the government. Through a system of penalty assessments, regulatory agencies deter future violations of laws helping to guarantee fair and equitable treatment to all businesses. Penalties also acknowledge the social debt owed to those who obey the law. It is fundamentally unfair to allow a violator to retain a competitive or economic advantage from breaking the law. In addition, the government cannot deter violations unless the violators are convinced that they have something to lose when they get caught.

When the regulated community sees that inspections and enforcement actions are fair and consistent, they perceive the assurance of fairness and the need to comply. It also tells them the enforcement process is not open to favoritism or bargaining for special treatment. Ideally, the response should be swift so the consequences are not evaded by excuses or the delay of lengthy negotiations.

Historically, enforcement based on deterrence has been the critical factor in motivating the regulated community toward environmentally responsible behavior. This results in the regulatory agencies devoting significant portions of their resources to this approach. Through rigorous inspection, detection of violations, and the resulting sanctions and penalties, offenders are forced to correct violations and are discouraged from future noncompliance. Under the deterrence approach, it is assumed that the more inspections conducted and enforcement actions taken, the greater the deterrent effect — and so the greater the level of compliance and environmental protection that will be achieved.

It is increasingly difficult to achieve significant levels of compliance through enforcement actions alone. Both the number of environmental requirements and the number of regulated entities continue to grow, while the resources available to assure compliance through enforcement actions continue to shrink under pressure to cut government spending. Though the number of regulated facilities nationwide has more than doubled in the last ten years, many state enforcement budgets have remained essentially flat when adjusted for inflation. For example, in New York, the number of regulated polluters has almost doubled to 19,000 in the last decade, but the number of inspections has remained about the same.[2] Although this trend would suggest a greater reliance on compliance promotion, implementation success will always rely on a foundation of "traditional" enforcement actions.

CHAPTER 2

THE JOB

Field personnel have the frontline job in implementing and enforcing environmental laws and regulations. A significant amount of time may be spent investigating the complaints that people report to an environmental regulatory agency. If one is not out conducting an inspection, you would likely be on the phone, taking down complaints or explaining the laws to people. In my experience with the State of Maine Department of Environmental Protection, new complaints came in on a steady basis; faster than could be investigated. No matter how many you resolved more kept coming in. My caseload never seemed to get smaller. During my last full year as an investigator, I was assigned two hundred twenty new complaints across the six program areas under our authority.

At the time, Department policy was such that each and every complaint required a site visit. In order to investigate a large number of complaints over a vast territory (four of us covered a region of approximately three thousand square miles), it was more efficient to group together several inspections and spend a day in one general area. Having to group complaints caused delays in getting out to see what was going on, but it was not possible or practical to jump in the car after every call unless it was an emergency; it was often days or weeks later before I could get into the field to investigate.

After escaping from the office, and out on an inspection, it is important to gather evidence to determine if any activities fall under the department's jurisdiction. Inspections are the government's main tool for officially assessing compliance. An inspection is an examination into the environmental affairs of a single regulated site and/or facility, to see whether it is in compliance with environmental requirements.

During the course of an inspection, it is crucial to observe and document what's happening and where (are ecologically sensitive areas affected?). This includes interviewing people who work on the site, obtaining their statements, reviewing and copying records, taking samples (i.e. water) for analysis at the lab, taking photographs and notes. It may be possible to size up the situation in one brief visit and determine if the activity is a violation or not. Typically, larger sites require more study. It may be necessary to check local or state records to determine the site's history and identify the owner(s). In addition, other agencies may have to become involved. The technical expertise of a geologist or biologist might be required to verify relevant facts. This will require setting up an appointment to meet with specialists and show them around the site. Working within a bureaucracy, your priorities are not always going to match those of the people you rely on, so this can mean a long wait for supporting services needed to build a case. Using the evidence, a determination must be made whether any laws have been broken. If laws have been broken, the next steps are to develop the enforcement case and negotiate an appropriate settlement to resolve the violation.

One way to resolve a violation is through a consent agreement/ order. A consent agreement is an out-of-court settlement among the alleged violator and the government. Every case involving a consent agreement requires close coordination with the attorney general. The attorney general is the chief law enforcement official for the state, and his or her decisions have a major influence over the strength of the environmental enforcement program in the state. The attorney general also has responsibility for suing violators, at the request of state environmental agencies.

An agreement is the preferred means of resolving violations because it is quicker and less complex than presenting a case in court, and the outcome is certain. If a judge decides a case there is always the possibility that a penalty and/or restoration measures may not be imposed. However, it is an agreement that all parties enter into voluntarily. The investigator must convince the violator, as well as your superiors[3], and the assistant attorney general assigned to the case, that the defendant is being treated fairly and it is in everyone's interest to settle. In doing so, you must demonstrate that the violation and impacts are worthy of everyone's time and energy, and the penalty and restoration measures are appropriate.

During negotiations the discussion always turns to the justification for the penalty amount. When trying to take money from people you must be able to explain it logically and reasonably. You can be sure when defendants have attorneys representing them, if they are any good, they will know the history of similar case settlements. If there is no consistency among the settlements, and in the manner in which you explain their violation, you can be accused of being arbitrary and capricious in your enforcement of the law, which will undermine your case.

Penalty calculation[4] is generally based upon a series of criteria: environmental impacts; cause of violation; number and nature of previous violations; cooperation in correcting the violation and minimizing damage; and potential for recurrence.[5]

The establishment of a figure could be perceived as somewhat subjective and dependent upon the opinion of the investigator. Often we would look to similar cases and add or subtract money depending on if the environmental damage was worse or not. In my experience, the guidelines gave you a figure that became a starting point for negotiations. However, when negotiating you have to keep in mind that if the penalty is too low, there will be no incentive to deter future violations; for the violator it will become a cost of doing business. If the defendant feels the penalty to be too high they will refuse to settle. Then you must decide if it is appropriate to pursue action in court.

Due to large caseloads, some violations will be more aggressively pursued than others. You must be selective because negotiating a consent agreement or taking someone to court can be a long drawn out process that takes away from the time you have to investigate new complaints. Even though the state has jurisdiction over a particular project it may not be necessary or appropriate to take formal action. Instead, it is important to use "enforcement discretion;" whereby parties reach a mutually agreeable solution that achieves compliance with the law. This may be used in a situation where work started without the proper permits, but there did not appear to have been any significant environmental damage. Under these circumstances it is agreed that no additional work take place until a permit is obtained.

The decision for determining when to use either enforcement discretion, or formal action will depend on the strength of the evidence. If the violation is easy to define and present, it could be aggressively pursued. In the best of circumstances an investigator finds the violation occurring during the inspection. Otherwise, it may be necessary to piece together what happened after-the-fact, from scanty evidence, which can result in a weak case. In some situations the case may be good enough to settle with a consent agreement, but not go to court.

I found that as the case developed, the attitude of the defendant could play a role in how it was handled. In some cases, assessing a fine may be unnecessary if people are cooperative. In contrast, individuals who are hostile may just make it tougher on themselves. In conjunction with one's attitude, whether or not someone was fined could also be influenced by how flagrant the violation is perceived to have been. If someone was caught "in the act" and you had a really strong case, it did not really matter what they were like, you could always go to court and they could explain themselves to a judge. If it was a technical violation, with little environmental damage, and the defendant was uncooperative, it could go either way. Since it was not possible to pursue everything, you need to prioritize and focus your efforts where there is the greatest impact.

An important part of the process in selecting a case for enforcement action is the discussion between an investigator and their supervisor. How the investigator explains the evidence greatly determines the manner in which to proceed with a case. A case is more likely to be pursued if there is strong evidence such as photographs or lab results which illustrate significant details of a violation. On the other hand, if there is little physical evidence, and little enthusiasm is demonstrated, the case may be passed over. Other factors which may influence the pursuit of a case include whether the defendant has a history of violations. If there were prior violations it was more likely that formal action would be taken. If another case was pending the current complaint could be included. Finally, significant public scrutiny by either private citizens and/or the press regarding a particular situation may force formal action on a minor case which probably would not have been pursued due to the insignificance of the environmental impacts.

Publicity could also be a tool used to the agency's advantage. Businesses seek to avoid adverse publicity and take care to try and preserve their environmentally friendly image. Locally profiled cases tend to raise the public awareness of the laws and deter others from committing a similar violation. Even stories of cases passed by word-of-mouth within the community are valuable: Industry knowledge is heightened in regards to applicable regulations for future projects prompting companies to inquire about the jurisdiction of environmental laws during a project's planning stage. In addition, past violators will become another set of eyes and file complaints about others doing the same things for which they were prosecuted. They rightly justify reporting their competitors due to the potential for them to take unfair advantage of not complying with the law.

One of the great rewards of the job was finding a clear cut violation and taking charge of the situation in order to fix it. With a solid case, you could negotiate from a position of strength and work aggressively for compliance. However, you only have that strength if your superiors support you and back you up if your actions are questioned. The first reaction of many violators when telling them they cannot do something, or have done it wrong, is to go over your head to either, your superiors including the governor's office, or to their legislators. This is why the relationship you have with your immediate supervisor and your credibility throughout the organization is so important. If there is no mutual respect or confidence, then you are on your own, which won't allow you to achieve much success.

Without mutual respect I would not feel comfortable in taking a controversial case. Why bother to put yourself in a potentially stressful situation if your superiors are going to cave-in? I was fortunate to have great support from my immediate supervisor. I recall him believing so strongly, in the defense of the actions of one of my colleagues concerning the pursuit of a particular case, that he yelled into the phone to his superiors "We'll all quit and go sell pencils on the street before we drop it." The alleged violation was so flagrant that he believed that if we dropped this case why bother pursuing any others.

The higher up the chain of command you go, into the ranks of political appointments, your support may not be dependable, and could potentially be erratic. This could likely be due to factors such as any ideological bent the appointee may have and their being subject to pressures of serving at the leisure of the governor. However, it may be as basic as not understanding the investigator's perspective because they had never been in the field, or even worked in the department before. In addition, field offices may be located in separate cities or towns from the headquarters so there is no opportunity for daily contact with the organization's leadership.

Gaining this respect, and their confidence, is earned through your actions in the field and in the office. It is very important to keep supervisors informed of the status of cases every step of the way to insure agreement on the course of action and that there are no unexpected surprises. For example, make sure your superiors agree it is appropriate to pursue a consent agreement. That way, when an irate violator calls the governor's office and it gets back to your supervisor, they can say they are familiar with the case and approve the course of action.

How you conduct yourself in the field will always filter back to your superiors as well. In addition to my immediate supervisor, who I had daily contact with, my superiors included the Director of the Land Bureau, the Commissioner of the Department, and the Board of Environmental Protection. They can gauge your performance by the feedback they get from those you interact with, whether they are defendants or colleagues in government. Respect from the public, and regulated community, does not come with a government I.D. You have to understand the different perspectives you will encounter and balance that with your responsibilities. Your actions should not give the defendant leverage for undermining your credibility and focusing discussions on "process" issues instead of the violations and resultant environmental damage. For example, property owners and potential violators frequently do not want people, particularly government officials, wandering around their property like they own it. Even though some statutes granted access to private property (not including residences) to conduct inspections, to neutralize the issue, I would make a point of asking for permission to be on the property any way. Not all complainants are necessarily on your side either. Some citizens' concerns may not center on the environment but rather nuisances such as traffic or dust, or that they thought somebody was getting away with something they could not. Nevertheless, they want rapid response and quick resolution to their complaint.

The investigator must recognize it is impossible to make everyone happy. In fact, you will make many of them angry, especially if you are delaying projects or interfering with business decisions where people have committed money. Dealing with people, explaining yourself and your position, and communicating that they are being treated fairly are important. If they are getting fined, and cannot move forward on their project, or it takes extra money, it makes your job easier if they feel they are not being singled out. As these situations show, the job can be thankless.

What makes the job rewarding is a great feature of public service: the large amount of responsibility given to individuals. In an entry level position as an investigator, you can be responsible for enforcing state or federal laws and interacting on a daily basis with local officials, businessmen, and the legal community. If I discovered a violation I made a point to call the president or one of the officers of the company. You may also enjoy wide latitude in prioritizing your work load and balancing your schedule between the office and fieldwork. A substantial benefit of these responsibilities was the opportunity to spend many hours outdoors exploring forests, wetlands, lakes, the coast, and then being able to see the direct result of your efforts to preserve those areas.

CHAPTER 3

STREAMS AND BROOKS

Rivers are ecologic systems, with the main stem, tributaries, riparian areas and floodplains as interdependent parts. In order to preserve water quality, as well as fish and wildlife habitat, the tributary streams and brooks, which are their foundation must be protected. If impacts of development were restricted to those causing them, perhaps the government regulation of activities affecting streams would not be necessary. With a medium such as water, which flows across private and political boundaries, this is not likely.

Many factors shape the character of a stream as it progresses from its headwaters to its mouth: the topography, the amount of water being transported, its temperature and chemistry. These in turn influence the vegetation, the animals, the bottom sediments and the shape of the channel.

There is more to a stream than water. The stream is enriched by a wide variety of animals and plants that live along or within its course. The kinds of animals and plants found in a stream change from its upper reaches to the broader downstream stretches.

The base of the food chain in the stream, as on land, is plants. But unlike forests, the stream does not rely directly on the energy of the sun (through photosynthesis) to generate its own plant life. Small streams are often too shady or too turbulent to support much microscopic algae or to allow larger plants to take root. Most of the plants in the stream actually fall into it. Plant litter tumbles in from the edge or from above, supplying essential food and nutrients to the stream ecosystem.

The condition of a stream's water will determine what can live in it. The quality of the water is the result of a combination of factors including its source, temperature, dissolved oxygen, and the nature of any contaminants. All of these factors are influenced by what happens in the stream's watershed and the water as it flows through it.

The color of a stream's water gives clues to what it has come in contact with: rainwater, groundwater or snowmelt run clear. The tannin from pine needles may stain the water to resemble tea. Turbidity - a cloudiness resembling a light cup of coffee -usually indicates the presence of sediments from erosion. The effect is caused by the scattering of light passing through the water as the fine soil particles are held in suspension by the turbulence of the current. If not controlled, land use activities can cause surface erosion, and subsequent turbidity, resulting in serious in-stream problems. The net result of erosion and turbidity on stream life depends on its severity and duration.

Various species of fish spend all or part of their lives in stream waters with their eggs developing within the bottom gravel. The eggs of salmon and trout, buried in streambed gravel, must remain for one to four months in silt-free water if they are to successfully hatch.

Where filter feeders (i.e. caddisflies) are common, the silt dilutes the nutritive value of their organic food particles and can weaken the population providing less food for fish. The fish need clear water for sighting prey; they must also defend and move around their territories by sight. Excess sediments not only reduce water clarity, they can also harm the gills of fish and aquatic insects or even ruin spawning beds. Gills are especially vulnerable to excess sediments, which can clog them directly or can irritate them into secreting so much mucous that the gill is unable to extract oxygen from the water.

Just as the level of turbidity in a stream can influence what lives in it, so does the water temperature. Plants and animals that live in the stream are completely surrounded by water, and so their "climate" depends on water temperature rather than air temperature. In fact, since fish and aquatic insects are cold-blooded, their body temperature adjusts to the temperature of the water they inhabit. Their metabolism and growth rate are regulated by the water temperature. If the water heats up too much – as it may in summer when water levels are low and the stream passes through unshaded areas – fish and insect respiration will speed up and demand more oxygen. Water in shaded streams may be many degrees cooler than the air above it, yet heat up (10 degrees or more) when passing through a clearing. The warmed water may be suddenly re-cooled downstream by either colder tributaries or springs.

For any given temperature there is a limit to the amount of oxygen that the water can hold in solution. The cooler the water, the more dissolved oxygen it can hold. In addition to temperature, the concentration of dissolved oxygen in the stream depends on the amounts taken out of the water by respiring and decaying organisms, and put back by physical aeration and photosynthesis. Still or slow-moving water gets some oxygen from the air above it. But in still water, only the upper layers receive much dissolved oxygen, while the bottom layer can be depleted by the respiration of animals. Water rushing over rocks and falls is aerated. Plants add oxygen to the water during day light as a byproduct of photosynthesis, but they also deplete it as they respire at night, and require even more as they decay.

Just as we depend on oxygen in the air, instream creatures depend on oxygen that is dissolved in the water. Water never contains large amounts of oxygen: the atmosphere contains twenty three percent oxygen, whereas even oxygen saturated water contains less than one percent. And so small losses or gains can be critical to instream animals. Heating the stream by removing shade trees or by holding it behind a dam, will cause its water to lose oxygen and may make it unfit for some fish. This is a primary reason why large active fish like salmon and trout, which need large amounts of oxygen, are restricted to cool waters. As the water temperature rises their metabolism demands more oxygen, but there is less available in solution. In summer, large rivers naturally warm to temperatures exceeding the limit for trout. This is due to their width which permits a large surface area to be directly heated by the sun. It is the small narrow stream with shading provided by a shore canopy which enables many trout to survive. Without these cool streams for refuge, a riverine system's trout population would be severely restricted if not eliminated.

From the air, the edges of a stream appear as bright green tracks furrowed into the forest floor. That's because grasses, shrubs, and trees flourish in the damp, fertile soil of the banks and floodplains that border the stream. This is the riparian zone, a protective margin of vegetation that keeps the water clear and cool for the instream creatures.

In addition to raising the temperature of the water, clearing vegetation, including the shore land tree canopy can increase stream flows. Flows accelerate because there is less obstruction to the water as it moves through the watershed. Stream flows depend not only on the amount of precipitation in a stream's watershed, but also on the surrounding soils and vegetation. Rainwater infiltrates the topsoil, unless the ground is already saturated from previous rainfall. Some of this groundwater will be drawn up by trees and other vegetation to be evaporated back in the air; the rest moves slowly through the soil and is gradually released into the stream channel. The vegetative cover of the entire watershed is important in aiding resistance to surface erosion and reducing sediments entering the streams. Replacing natural area with paved surfaces increases runoff and minimizes organic inputs by allowing all the rainwater to reach streams without delay. An increase in flow can cause stream bed erosion and scouring which is physically disruptive to bottom organisms and fish spawning and nursery areas. Undisturbed stream side vegetative buffer strips of one hundred feet, or more, are perhaps the least expensive and most effective means to prevent impacts and maintain the health of streams and the rivers they feed into.

A result of the long term appreciation in the value of land is the eventual profitability in developing "marginal" property where it formerly was not economical to fill and grade a building lot with substantial amounts of off-site material. Typically, this meant the land was either in, or adjacent to, wetlands, stream or on a floodplain. The following cases illustrate the tension between development and the preservation of tributary streams.

BUILDING A STREAM CROSSING

A common source of information for agencies is anonymous citizen complaints. A typical springtime caller reported that a stream channel had been "redirected" in the process of constructing several new houses in the Topsham Gardens Subdivision.

The site was approximately thirty miles from the office so a couple of weeks passed before I was able to make a trip to the area. After making a couple of stops to sites with activities that the State did not have jurisdiction over, I found the entrance to the Subdivision. It was rather large and, from the appearance of the houses, had been built several years earlier. I passed three or four secondary roads and took a right onto Hanson Drive. After passing a dozen houses, the pavement ended and a fresh dirt road continued with a new home on either side. The yards had not been landscaped and remained just loose soil.

I parked the car and began to look around. At one time, a stream channel ran through the low area where the pavement now ended. Fill was brought in to establish house sites and a road crossing. In doing so, a thirty six inch corrugated aluminum pipe was placed in the channel and extended downstream between two houses so more soil could be placed over it to level the yard. A significant length of the stream channel was buried and now ran through the pipe, another section had been diverted. They also buried a small tributary that ran perpendicular to the main channel to level off the property to put in more houses. See Figure I for site plan. One new house and the foundation for another were already in place.

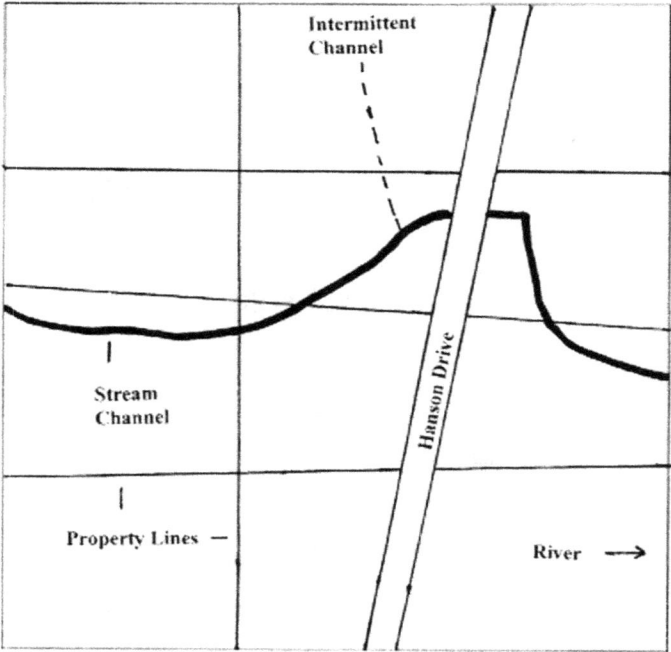

Figure I − Hanson Drive Crossing Site of the Tributary of the Androscoggin River

To document the activities on the site, and summarize the potential violation, I took several pictures and paced the length of total stream channel affected. I carried a one hundred foot steel tape to measure distances and to calculate the size of affected areas. However, when really large distances are involved it is more convenient to pace it out to obtain an estimate. Before going in the field, you measure out one hundred feet and count off the number of steps it takes you to cover it. After doing this a couple of times you will have a good idea how many steps it takes you to cover a known distance. Then when you go out in the field you just count off the steps. First, I paced it out to obtain a ball-park figure and estimated that well over two hundred feet of channel was altered. Next, I measured with the tape where the pipes were installed and the length of new channel and determined at least two hundred forty five feet was affected. It may have been more but the site was so disturbed it was difficult to determine where the original stream course was located.

It is generally a good idea to walk upstream, as well as downstream, of the affected area to get an idea of what the characteristics of the ecosystem are and be able to provide a context for how the activities impact the environment. Walking downstream through the woods, the stream was largely undisturbed for a couple hundred feet and then flowed through a culvert under a two lane road. On the other side of the road it became progressively bigger and flowed down a large ravine. After consulting a map I determined it to be a tributary of the Androscoggin River. Upstream, the original subdivision had been built over the old channel. Walking back through the subdivision it was clear that the stream was redirected through ditches in various yards as well as the occasional pipe. There were no buffer strips between the stream and lawns. In the woods upstream of the subdivision, the channel, although smaller, flowed freely from its source which was a small wetland. After writing up a description of the site and drawing a crude map showing where the pictures had been taken, I returned to the office.

To provide for necessary activities near streams, the law contained an exemption from state regulation for the construction of crossings that affected less than fifty feet of channel. In consultation with my supervisor, we decided to pursue formal enforcement action, including the assessment of penalties and restoration, because well over the fifty feet allowed to construct a crossing had been obliterated. If the developer had properly designed and built the crossing it is possible it may have qualified for an exemption. However, the majority of the alterations were for the "aesthetics" of being able to install larger lawns. In addition to easily being able to illustrate that it was a violation, there were significant amounts of exposed soils that could erode into the stream and cause additional damage if not stabilized.

One potential complication to the case may have been the status of the earlier part of the subdivision. It was obvious the developer of the existing houses had also altered the stream during those construction activities. To prosecute the current construction, and not the former, would be a double standard that may provide the defendant with an argument of unfair application of the law. After consulting with the town office, it was determined that the earlier construction had been completed prior to the passage of the law; therefore, the State only had jurisdiction over the more recent activities.

My next step was to contact the violator to inform them of the findings of the investigation and get their side of the story. In order to locate the owner of the project I called the realtor whose name was listed on a for-sale sign. After introducing myself, I explained that I had been out to Hanson Drive in response to a complaint. He asked who complained. I told him it was anonymous.

In this instance it actually was, but even if someone left their name, unless it was another public official, we did not divulge that information as it will discourage people from reporting to us, as well as divert discussion away from the violation. At the time, I thought the complainant was probably one of the current residents who was disappointed by the loss of some of the surrounding trees and the addition of new neighbors.

I went on to explain it appeared they violated State law by extending Hanson Drive and filling and grading the area for new house sites. Approximately two hundred forty five feet of channel of two tributaries of the Androscoggin River had been buried in a pipe and redirected. A review of State records indicated a permit had not been obtained.

The realtor explained the history of the site to me: most of the subdivision had been built years ago. He and a partner recently bought the last few undeveloped lots from the original developer and they were in the process of building single family homes. They had gone to the town office and received all local approvals and assumed none others were necessary.

They wanted to maintain and complete the alterations so I informed him of the necessity to obtain a permit by filing an "after-the-fact" application. In the meantime, exposed soils adjacent to the stream should be covered with mulch and bales of hay or siltation fencing placed adjacent to the channel to form a barrier to prevent soil from washing into the water. No additional fill should be placed adjacent to the stream or in the area where it used to flow unless a permit is obtained. These measures, would hopefully, limit erosion and resultant turbidity in the stream. I immediately followed our conversation with a letter that summarized my findings and outlined the next steps which included the drafting of a consent agreement.

By late summer, a consent agreement was forwarded to the developers which levied a penalty of twenty five hundred dollars and contained provisions to restore the stream if their permit application was denied. I requested a response in two weeks.

As the summer was ending, the permit analyst who would be coordinating the review of the application contacted me and wanted to meet at the site to familiarize himself with the project. During the visit I noticed that additional fill covering an area of approximately six thousand square feet had been placed next to the stream channel. A review of the documentation from my previous visit, which I brought with me, confirmed this. Due to the difficulty in being able to schedule time to revisit sites, accurate documentation is essential. If I did not have reliable records I would be unable to prove additional work had been conducted.

In response to the agreement, the developers forwarded a letter stating several reasons why they did not want to enter into one including: the affected area was not a stream as defined by the statute, the work done had actually "improved" it, and the State should not hold them liable since the town planning board did not inform them State permits were necessary. Since they had a lot of money invested in the project they did not want to sign anything that would jeopardize their plans.

My written response addressed each of their points: the stream had defined banks and a mineral bottom thus meeting the statutory definition; it was difficult to see how burying it was an improvement; and it is not the planning board's responsibility to inform them if a project is under the jurisdiction of State regulations. To exert pressure on them to settle, I also explained that I had recently inspected the site and determined additional work, in violation of the law, had been conducted since my June inspection. I reminded them of our earlier conversation and correspondence instructing them not to undertake additional activities unless and until a permit was obtained. I emphasized that this latest violation was not included in the penalty calculation but could be if the agreement was not signed.

In November, the permit application was denied because the project would cause unreasonable erosion, interfere with the natural flow of water and habitat for aquatic life. It was also found that the small tributary was so damaged by prior development that little, if any, benefit would be gained by its restoration. However, a State biologist determined the channel, downstream of the crossing and the most recent work, supported aquatic life and should be restored. The biologist recommended reclaiming the section buried for yard improvement, which totaled about one hundred feet of stream channel.

I modified the agreement assessing a seventeen hundred fifty dollar penalty, required the removal of about seventy five feet of pipe, and restoration of the channel and revegetation of the banks. The penalty was lowered because there is always some room built in for negotiation and in recognition that the previous construction, not their activities, had been responsible for reducing the value of one tributary. Before the end of the year, they signed the agreement and paid the penalty. Since the permit was denied, the project was approved by the consent agreement as it recognized the alterations and stipulated certain corrective actions. The following spring, the contractor indicated he had removed the pipe and planted vegetation. A follow-up inspection revealed the work had been completed.

The case demonstrates the value of reaching an agreement satisfactory to these businessmen and the State. The developers were able to build the road, the crossing, and develop all of the house lots they had planned to, while the State was able to minimize the impacts to the stream by restoring the part of the channel capable of supporting aquatic life and reestablishing a vegetative buffer.

TRIBUTARY OF LONG CREEK I

One March day, I received a call that someone allegedly placed fill in a stream at a construction equipment dealership on County Road in Westbrook. In April, I was able to inspect the site and meet with the owner. I went to the place of business unannounced, introduced myself, and explained to him that is was my understanding that someone had placed fill adjacent to a tributary of Long Creek that bordered his property. I asked if I could look around. He agreed and escorted me around the property. His business involved the sale and rental of heavy construction equipment such as bulldozers and backhoes. We walked through the garage to the rear of the property where several pieces of machinery were lined up for perspective customers. Behind the merchandise there was a stream that was a couple of feet wide that had a strong flow. Wetlands were associated with some reaches of the stream as evidenced by the presence of cattails.

Fresh earth had been pushed next to the water and was washing into the channel. The owner explained that he had wanted to expand the area where he parked the machinery and a customer actually did the work so he could try out a particular piece of equipment. I paced the length of channel that was disturbed and determined it to be approximately two hundred feet. I also noted that the stream ran through several commercial subdivisions before its confluence with Long Creek so it had varying levels of protection by adjacent buffer strips. Some areas were undisturbed with wide buffer strips of natural vegetation while others were highly developed that afforded little protection.

I informed the owner this work was a violation of State law unless he had a permit. He said he did not. I also explained that there was a strong possibility that the Department may take formal enforcement action because, as with building a structure, you need a permit to work in such close proximity to a stream. I assumed since he was familiar with the construction business he could probably relate to the necessity of getting permits. I left him materials that explained the law and permit requirements.

After discussing the facts with my colleagues we decided to pursue a consent agreement because it was a strong case and the watershed was under heavy development pressure. We hoped the attendant publicity would caution others to be more careful in the pursuit of their projects.

A few days after my inspection, I called the property owner and explained we would be assessing his company a penalty for the violation. I also asked him to pull the material back from the stream and to stabilize it with vegetation. He asked with what. I suggested putting in a buffer strip of white pine trees so, in the future, perspective customers would have a natural barrier that would keep them away from the stream. I followed this conversation with a letter detailing it and requested that the work be complete by May 1.

He agreed to the remediation and said he would take care of it quickly. In early May, I received a call saying that he had completed the restoration work. I was able to drive by the property and saw the exposed soils had been pulled back and a new row of white pine trees had been planted along the embankment.

As demonstrated by his good faith efforts in quickly performing the remedial work I requested, it turned out the owner was very cooperative. He even called me sometime later to look at another piece of property he owned with a stream running through it. He wanted a determination whether some work he planned to do needed a permit or not. I eventually forwarded an agreement that assessed a seven hundred fifty dollar penalty. The agreement included a description of how the remediation efforts had already been completed. He agreed and we had a final sign off by the State in September.

CHAPTER 4

FRESHWATER WETLANDS, LAKES AND PONDS

Wetlands are areas where water is the primary factor control-ling plant and animal life. Wetlands are transitional habitats that occur between upland and aquatic environments. The water table is at or near the surface of the ground, or is completely covered by shallow water that may be several feet deep. There are three major categories of freshwater wetlands: palustrine, lacus-trine, and riverine. Palustrine means marshy; wetland areas with-in this category include marshes, swamps, and bogs. Lacustrine wetlands are associated with lakes; and riverine with rivers and streams.

Marshes may begin as shallow lakes or depressions that gradu-ally fill in with decomposed vegetation. Marshes are character-ized by soft-stemmed emergent plants such as cattails. Emergents are plants that grow with their stems partly in and partly out of water. Shallow marshes are those with up to six inches of water, deep marshes have two to three feet of water. Seasonal fluctuations in the water level may occur: the water may rise with the spring rains and recede during the drier summer months. In the deeper marshes, floating and submerged aquatics, such as water lilies and pondweeds, may be common with cattails, arrowheads, and other emergents common in shallow areas.

Unlike marshes, swamps are dominated by woody plants; namely trees and shrubs. Some wooded swamps develop from marshes, while others do not result from a transition of this sort, but originate directly in poorly drained depressions. Swamps can be forested with either hardwood trees, such as red maple; or by softwood evergreens, such as cedars, firs, and spruces. Beneath the trees a variety of wetland shrubs – including Highbush Blueberry and Sweet Pepperbush may be present. Willows, alders, shrubby dogwoods and button bush form shrub swamps.

Bogs occur primarily in formerly glaciated areas of the Northeast. Bogs are peat lands, usually lacking an overlying layer of mineral soils. The substrate - peat – is formed by the building up and gradual decomposition of plant material; this accumulation is especially favored in highly acidic, poorly drained areas where decomposing bacteria cannot thrive. Peat forms a floating mat of vegetation over the water, and can accumulate in deposits thick enough to walk on. Insect eating plants such as Sundews and Pitcher Plants are commonly found on this mat.

Wetlands play many roles: controlling floodwater, recharging groundwater, filtering pollutants; and as habitat for wildlife including waterfowl and fish. They can serve as temporary storage basins, reducing the destructive potential of severe floods.

It has long been recognized that aquatic systems have a certain self-cleansing ability. If sewage is added upstream, the organic level will be considerably reduced by the time the waters have traveled several miles downstream. Dilution is one reason, but another is the ability of aquatic organisms such as algae to take up minerals and break down organic matter. This process will not work if more sewage is added than the system can process. Runoff from agricultural land often puts excess nitrogen and phosphorus – the components of fertilizers – into rivers and lakes. Wetlands can absorb some of these nutrients and thus improve water quality. Most of the excess settles into the sediments and can be used by wetland plants at a later date. The portion that is not used may be flushed out by spring flooding.

Offering yet another level of diversity in wetlands habitats are lakes and ponds, which are standing bodies of water ranging in size from less that one acre to several thousand acres. The primary difference between a lake and pond is size. Lakes are usually deep, large bodies of water, and ponds are typically smaller and shallower. In addition, ponds usually have water of uniform temperature, whereas that of a lake changes with depth (warmer at the surface, cooler at the bottom). These lacustrine environments often include areas of shallow water along their margins, where marshes and swamp forests may develop. Beyond the shoreline, one encounters deepwater habitats, where rooted aquatic plants may be absent because of a lack of light. Lakes and ponds may be of glacial origin, but many are man-made.

Every lake is unique. Because lakes vary in size, shape, depth, and surrounding watershed, some lakes are able to support more and different kinds of life than others. For example, many shallow lakes have always lacked the deep, cold water necessary for salmon and lake trout to survive. But regardless of size or shape, all lakes go through a similar aging process. Over time, sediment builds up on a lake bottom. If enough sediment builds up, the lake can become shallower causing a change in fish species and increases in plant life. Eventually, a lake could fill in completely and become a swamp or peat bog.

A lake is a complex, interrelated system which can absorb only so much change. Many factors contribute to the composition of a lake including: water depth, wind and currents; surface area; light; available nutrients; and local geology. Although no two lakes are completely identical in their composition and wildlife, they all have a fragile nature.

The existing natural shoreline is almost always stable because it has been subjected to thousands of years of water, wind, and ice action. These forces have changed the original shoreline to a stable form. Any change now is almost sure to make for less stability. Over-intensive development, with structures too close together or too close to the shore, can lead to shoreline erosion.

Due to their tranquil settings, lakes and ponds are frequently subject to heavy development pressure that may destroy the qualities that attracts so many people to them in the first place. The degree of impact of any alterations will depend on the character of the lake. Cumulative effects may not be apparent for some time, especially if the changes are small and the lake is large. Harmful changes include filling, either directly or by erosion/beach construction along the shore. The shoreline areas are important because their shallow weedy and rocky areas provide basic support for life that inhabits the lake including: spawning areas for some species of warm water fish (i.e. bass), habitat for some adult fish (i.e. large mouth bass, pickerel), and feeding areas and protection for young waterfowl. Construction of permanent docks, piers, and breakwaters removes habitat and may alter current flows resulting in water stagnation or shoreline erosion. In addition to these activities, dredging can reduce a lake's habitat value and the resultant siltation degrades water quality which can lead to eutrophication.

Eutrophication is the gradual increase in a lake's ability to support plant growth as a result of increases in nutrients, particularly phosphorus, concentrations. To a limited extent this process occurs naturally, but it is greatly accelerated by increased development and other land uses in the watersheds. During construction, erosion can be a major source of phosphorus. In general, the more phosphorus imported into the lake, the more algae will grow. If too much algae is present, as it decomposes it will deplete the dissolved oxygen available in the water which in turn will adversely impact fish and other organisms. If a lot of algae is present it also reduces the visibility under water. In extreme cases the water actually appears green and this reduces the lake's value in terms of aesthetics and recreational use. You know it is bad when you are standing in the shallows and you cannot see your feet.

Rivers and streams run into, through, and out of freshwater wetlands, lakes and ponds. A river, once polluted, can recover its former water quality when the offending industrial or municipal discharges are removed. A lake, however, may never fully recover. The reason for the difference is that rivers continually flush themselves of sediments and pollution; while lake water drains very slowly, and sediments on the lake bottom can act as a storehouse of pollutants.

The characteristics of wetlands, lakes, and ponds have important economic properties that should be protected. Millions of Americans hunt the waterfowl that breed, nest, and feed in wetlands. Millions more enjoy fishing as a sport. In addition to residing in the lakes and ponds, many freshwater fish are directly connected to the wetlands. Several species require areas of shallow water for breeding and feeding for some part of their life cycle. Fish retreat to these areas to avoid predators, which are generally less common in shallow waters. Pristine lake waters add beauty and diversity to the landscape, provide recreational opportunities throughout the seasons, and can be an important source of drinking water. For example, in Maine, the largest city in the State, Portland, depends on one of the State's largest lakes, Sebago, for its drinking water.

THE ICE POND

On a late fall day, I received a call from someone complaining about their neighbor setting off explosives in conjunction with some type of construction project. A builder was blasting a rock ledge out from an area next to his summer cottage. It shook the whole place and rocks were flying onto his property and hitting the house. I told him that we do not have jurisdiction over blasting and that he should check with the town office. I assumed that the builder would need some type of permit to use the explosives. The caller said he already checked with the town and they were not going to do anything. Besides, he also knocked down a dam, drained a pond, and was digging in the pond's bottom. This sounded more like something we handled. I wrote it up and turned it in to my supervisor. It's kind of like a lottery to see which complaints you end up with. Sometimes you take a complaint and write it up and say to yourself "I hope I don't get assigned that one." Dynamite was something I had not dealt with before. A couple of days later I found the complaint in my office mail box.

The site of the complaint was in Phippsburg, which is a town located on a peninsula in Casco Bay. It has an extensive rocky coastline typical of the Maine coast. The town's roads are narrow and the houses far apart. As you drive along, one minute you're going through rolling pine woodlands and the next you will be next to a cove, inlet, or mud flat. The site was located near the tip of the peninsula at West Point.

I took a right turn off of West Point Road, just beyond the Pine Grove Community Church, onto a single lane dirt road. Leaving the pavement, the road took an immediate dip to a stone bridge that acted as a dam to form a small pond to my left. The stream formed by the overflow from the dam ran off through a field of tall grass. The road continued up a small hill through a dark forest of large pine trees. I had to drive slowly to avoid the outcroppings of bedrock in the road. Breaking through the trees, the road went down towards an inlet and came to a dead end with a couple of summer cottages on either side. The two next to the water had their own docks. Beyond the end of the road, along the shore, was a small pier with a couple of commercial fishing boats.

I parked next to the green cottage at the end of the road. Since it was late fall it was boarded up. This was the one that belonged to the caller. Behind this cottage was a grass covered earthen dam. The dam had been breached and a small amount of water was flowing through it into a small channel that ran down to a corrugated aluminum pipe under the road which emptied into the inlet. I walked through the breach to see what was on the other side. The dam was about eight feet high, twelve feet thick and at least one hundred feet long.

Behind the dam was a long basin that must have held the water when the dam was whole. The ground was soft, saturated with water, and covered with grass. A short distance from the dam sat a large backhoe. It had been used to dig up a twenty by fifty foot square area. It was difficult to tell how deep the hole was since it had filled up with water. This pool was the source of water trickling through the breach in the dam. Upstream there was also a channel that flowed into the excavated area. From the direction of its source it appeared to be the stream I noticed crossing the stone bridge off the main road.

This seemed to be the type of activity the State had jurisdiction over. I took a couple of pictures and made some rough sketches of the site. See Figure 2. The next thing I had to do was determine what type of system it was in order to determine if any law had actually been broken. The location where the digging occurred could either be considered a pond, although all the water had been drained out, a freshwater wetland or a stream. I used the process of elimination to figure out our jurisdiction.

For a pond to be regulated by the State, if it is formed by a dam, it had to be greater than 30 acres in size. The basin was far too small; it was only three or four acres. So I needed to look at other criteria.

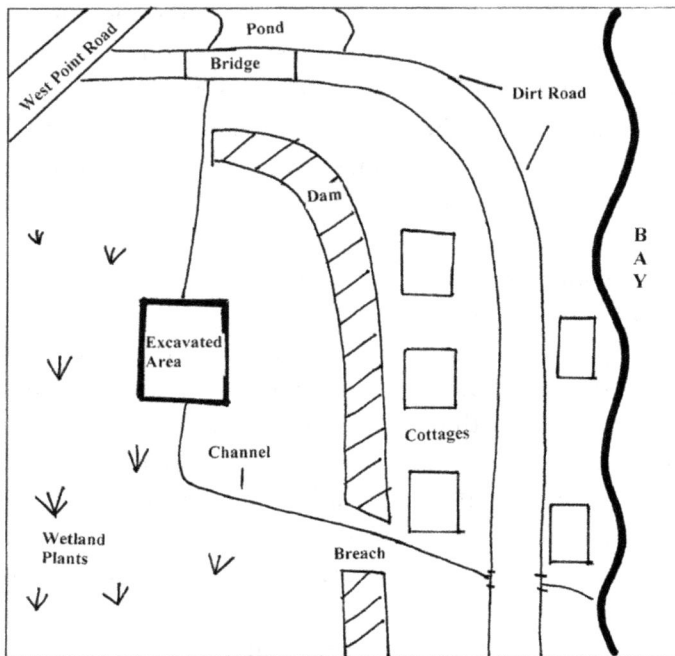

Figure 2 — West Pt. Road Site

A freshwater wetland was regulated by the State if it was ten or more acres in size. While the basin did not appear large enough I could not actually see the entire boundary of the wetland area. Water tolerant vegetation can be used to identify the wetland boundaries. Even though I could see most of the basin, wetlands may extend up along and go into the adjacent wooded areas. There could also be a hydraulic connection to adjacent areas via a stream channel.

If there is standing water and emergent vegetation, like cattails the boundary can be pretty obvious. But this is not always the case; often there are transition zones where wetland vegetation may be mixed with upland species as the topography slowly changes. There are also many types of grasses, shrubs, and trees that can be used to characterize a wetland. The potential combination of various plant types are numerous so many wetlands will look similar but with unique variations.

Delineating boundaries for even a small area of wetland is very time consuming as you have to identify individual plant species. This is where your botany skills come into play. Some plants like cattails are easy to recognize from a distance. But others may be more difficult as they are not so unique looking. For example, the field I was standing in was grass. To the untrained eye, it looks pretty much like any other grass. However, if it is a wetland certain types of grasses will be able to tolerate the water and others will not.

If you are not familiar with a particular plant you can possibly identify it by comparing its physical characteristics to a key or guide. The things you look for are the shape of the leaves, the pattern they are attached to the stem, the shape of the stem, and the flowers and fruit. This process is similar to taking apart a word to define it by its Latin root.

An additional level of difficulty can be added with the changing seasons: in the fall leaves and flowers are dried up or gone and in winter the landscape can be covered in snow. Identifying plants is a skill that takes practice to master. Just as learning a foreign language requires practice to gain fluency. You can even make flash cards for reference and to reinforce the images. We had a set of common wetland plants that were dried and pressed that were stored at the office so we could gather samples in the field and take them back for comparison.

I could have spent all day there walking the perimeter of the pond/wetland and try to identify the various plants. Some I recognized and some I did not. But I had some alternative tools to use. The State had developed a set of maps from aerial photographs of all the freshwater wetlands that were ten or more acres in size. This was a resource that would tell me if the State recognized the general area as a wetland. Even if it appears on the map you have to go out in the field to determine the boundaries. A review of the map indicated it was not such an area. That left the stream as an option for jurisdiction. There was a defined channel entering and exiting the excavated area.

While we could have pursued the alleged violation that the work commenced without the proper permits, we decided not to take formal enforcement action because there did not appear to have been any significant impacts from the excavations. We also took into account that the area was already altered by the construction of the dam many years ago. Instead we decided to ask the property owner that no additional work take place until a stream alteration permit was obtained. Our main concern was that the excavation not cause siltation that would flow into the coastal wetland area below the dam.

Having obtained the name of the property owner from the complainant, I called him and explained my investigation and belief that the project was subject to State regulation. He explained that he did not know any permits were necessary, but that he would not do additional work and would stop by my office the next chance he had. On a snowy day several weeks later I got a call from him saying that he was in town and would be coming by to see me with the plans for his project.

When he first arrived we exchanged pleasantries: he asked if I had attended the State University. I think he was looking for common ground to relate to me on and gain some empathy. Any way, he was very cordial and explained the history of the property which was rather interesting. The land that included the pond had been in his family for several generations. He actually lived in a house on the far side of the pond. The dam had been built about a hundred years ago to form the pond (known as No Name Pond). In the nineteenth century, during the wintertime, ice would be cut from the pond and loaded onto schooners which sailed into the inlet. After loading their cargo and packing it in straw, it would be transported to points south. It would be sold and stored in ice houses for use in the summer months.

Over the years, silt, mud, and detritus accumulated in the pond reducing its depth. At the end of the summer, when the water was low, it was only a couple of feet deep and became a stagnant breeding ground for mosquitoes and algae. It was his intention to drain the pond and dredge out the silt and mud to increase the depth of the basin. He would then repair the dam, refill the pond and possibly stock it with fish. The blasting became necessary because there was ledge blocking further drainage to the dam. While the standing water drained off when the dam was breached, the water table was so high that when they began digging, the hole quickly filled with water and made additional excavation difficult. A contractor friend of his, who he went to the University with, was providing the equipment in exchange for the material which could be used for fill or topsoil.

He agreed to apply for a permit and promised to stabilize the site and maintain erosion controls until he received it. This meant installing hay bale check dams and lining the outflow channel with rock. Until he removed more of the ledge there was little opportunity for much material to move very far and these measures would be sufficient. A follow up inspection showed he did a good job too.

A while later the complainant called me at the office to find out what happened. When I informed him that the necessary permits were being applied for and the goal was to increase the pond's depth and stock it with fish he sounded somewhat enthusiastic. He agreed it became buggy in the summer so it would definitely improve the enjoyment of his cottage.

As this situation shows, not every case is appropriate for pursuing formal enforcement action. Although some work was completed, little if any damage was evident. There may have been some siltation in the water but since no work was being conducted during my visit it was difficult to prove. If he wanted to challenge the stream alteration finding he could have argued that it was not a stream but a pond that was not under our jurisdiction: The channel was only there because he had breached the dam. If he fixed the dam the channel would disappear. In the alternative, we could go on to make the case that the channel below the dam was a stream and he would be putting material into that. But even then, that was created and altered many years ago.

In some cases, like this one, the site may not fit neatly into the definitions described in the law. You also don't necessarily know ecologically which would be the most productive or least destructive option to pursue. Is the best thing to dredge the area out or not? At one time, before the dam was built, there probably was a stream flowing through there, then after the dam was built the pond formed, and from its description was evolving into a wetland.

CHAPTER 5

COASTAL WETLANDS

Salt marshes are delicate ecosystems that cannot exist just any-where along a shoreline. It is impossible for them to develop along exposed seashores, for even moderate waves destroy their fragile structure. Nor can they grow far up in rivers, since the plants that are the basis for their biological economy require a salinity nearly equal to that of the ocean. Where then do they occur? Only along the shores of bays or in lagoons behind barrier islands, and only on terrain that is flat enough to allow their development.

Salt marshes build in shallow, quiet water, where sediment is permitted to drop out of suspension in the water and carpet the bottom. As the substrate rises to the level of the water's surface, grasses that are tolerant of salt water take hold and trap even more suspended particles, which become compacted as mud. Salt marsh-es are the products of tides, which flood their expanse twice a day, keeping them flat and level and drawing off the organic detritus that results from plant decay. Nutrients and minerals washed from the uplands or carried by streams which feed into the wetlands, add to the richness of the area. The tides then mix and redistribute all these nutrients throughout the shallows and into the sea.

On the Atlantic Coast, salt marshes are not common north of Cape Cod. Although a few can be found wherever condi-tions are right, along Maine's thirty five hundred mile coastline are found approximately seventeen thousand acres of salt marsh. These coastal wetlands account for only a tiny fraction of one percent of the State's total acreage. Geology and topography do not favor salt-marsh formation in the northern latitudes along the Atlantic Coast. Heavy glacial erosion sculpted deep river valleys, unlike the rivers of the South that never knew glacial action. It is almost impossible for river carried sediment to fill their fjord like mouths. Furthermore, the hard rock of northern coasts does not erode easily or grind down into fine sediments that settle as mud.

As with freshwater wetlands, plants provide the best means by which coastal wetlands and its boundaries can be identified, because they grow in specific locations depending on the amount of salt they can tolerate. As the tides go in and out, both the amount of salt (salinity) and temperature of their environment change rapidly. Salt tolerant wetland plants must be able to adapt to these quick changes and the number of plants which can do this is relatively few. As an investigator, familiarity with coastal wetland plants is another necessary skill area.

The typical wetland area, from tidal flats to the upland can be roughly divided into three zones: 1. Low marsh: this is the inter-tidal area that is subject to all phases of the tides, including the lowest, or "neap" tides. All the vegetation in this zone is covered by salt water twice a day. Spartina alterniflora, or salt marsh cord grass, dominates this low area. 2. High Marsh: this area is subject to tidal action several times during the month, particularly during periods of the new and full moon tides. High marsh plants include sea lavender; a black rush, juncus gerardi; and the dominant species, spartina patens. This thin salt hay grass may well cover sixty percent of the high marsh area. Salt meadows of spartina patens provide major nesting and feeding areas for birds, such as rails, sparrows, ducks, and red winged blackbirds. 3. Transitional Marsh: This is the area where upland meets coastal wetland. It is affected by only the maximum tides, and is the upper limit of plant species which can survive a salt environment. Plants here include the salt marsh sedge and the salt marsh aster.

Plants are the major producers in wetland areas, in their living as well as decaying forms. Living plants produce seeds and flowers directly eaten by animal life. Dead plants, fallen among the living, decay and are used by other organisms for food. Bacteria and other microscopic organisms reduce detritus to forms which can be used by plant and animal plankton as well as by larger animals.

Beyond the low marsh and along the banks of creeks which run through the marsh are mud flats vital to the shellfish population. Here, clams, mussels, and worms burrow in the mud. Crabs live in the mud and frequent the marsh for food. In tidal pools dotting the marsh are found specimens from the intertidal zone just beyond. They include small shrimp, minnows, and shellfish. Tidal creeks are the nursery and spawning area for many species of fish and shellfish, including crab and clam larvae, flounder, striped bass and menhaden. Nearly two thirds of all fish caught on the continental shelf have spent some portion of their lives in wetland areas.

Throughout history, coastal wetlands have long played an important role: Indians and early settlers used them for fishing and hunting. Later settlers built wharfs over them and harvested firewood and salt hay. In colonial times, town ordinances granted all inhabitants the common use of these areas for "free fishing and fowling." As time passed, the focus of the town shifted upland, away from the marsh areas. Individuals began to look at wetlands as their own property, and began to look for ways to adapt or "improve" wetlands for other uses. Only shellfish diggers and waterfowl hunters continued to utilize wetlands for their natural value, food. Today, many still think of wetlands as a wasteland with no usefulness at all. However, the value of wetlands for food production is tremendous; in fact, they are among the most naturally productive ecosystems in the world. The destruction of even a small wetland area can have a major effect on shellfish and finfish populations offshore. Dredging and removing sections of wetlands disrupts the food chain. Filling them in restricts tidal flushing and interferes with natural flood prevention. Finally, a coastal wetland serves as a protective buffer between land and sea. They act much like a great sponge, absorbing excess water during storms, cushioning the effects of waves and tidal action, limiting the danger of upland flooding.

Over seventy percent of the world's population lives in the coastal zone which causes the coastal zone to be a major center for transportation, commerce and recreation. At the same time, this vast region of the world is subject to multiple stresses including over fishing, species invasion, climate change and sea level rise and development. By restricting activities which harm wetlands, as dredging and filling do, the government provides a measure of protection for these valuable areas.

THE MARINA

Due to its rugged beauty, many of these fragile environments are subject to intense development pressures. Very early in the spring, before any leaves were even on the trees, I received a complaint concerning the possible filling of a coastal wetland near the mouth of the Saco River by Camp Ellis.

Camp Ellis was formerly a summer colony established on the beach in the late nineteenth century. More recently, many of the summer cottages have been converted into year round residences.

There had been a lot of construction in the area due to the installation of new sewer lines into the neighborhood. Since much of the work was in, and around, coastal wetlands and the beach area, the construction was being conducted under a State Permit.

I was responsible for making periodic site inspections to track the activity associated with the permit and make sure its conditions were followed. During the weeks the project was underway, the office received several calls concerning activity in the neighborhood, most of which turned out to be related to this public works construction.

I approached the beach area along Ferry Road. Shortly before reaching Camp Ellis there was a field containing equipment and pipe that was being stored for the sewer line project. I took a right there and headed down toward the River. I came to a house which also had construction equipment and materials surrounding it.

I parked the car and noticed a big guy with a beard preparing some tools near one of the pieces of equipment. I went over, introduced myself as being with the Department, and explained that I was investigating a complaint that work was being done along the River. I asked if I could look around the property. He told me to check with his father, but to be careful: "He was the old country." I was not sure what to make of that.

Now, a little more nervous than when I first arrived, I went to the house and rang the bell. A short old guy with a mustache answered the door. I again introduced myself and explained that we received a complaint that fill was being dumped into a wetland possibly on his property. He said it was true and would show me where. "Wow," I thought, "an admission of guilt right off the bat." We walked down a dirt road which ended in a marsh area along the River's edge. Sure enough, there were large piles of fresh soil in, and around, the wetland. He said he had a permit and would be happy to show it to me. I was somewhat skeptical. If he did have a permit, I thought our office would be aware of it and track it like we were the sewer project.

We went back to the house. He invited me inside while he went through his papers. He started discussing the history of his adventures with the State concerning the property and his plan to build a marina. He had that "here we go again" tone to his voice and "ready to fight" twinkle in his eye. He went through a lot over the years and would not stand for any more "officials" telling him what to do with his property. He did not raise his voice, nor was he sarcastic, while I was courteous and expressed curiosity concerning his previous travails. I let him do most of the talking: I found if you listen, especially without interrupting, people are usually forthcoming with information and often say too much. After about twenty minutes he produced a permit that allowed him to build a marina. It was issued seventeen years ago. A permit normally expired in two years. I did not say anything but took a copy, thanked him for his time, and went on my way.

Since he had previous encounters with State officials I figured I should do a little research on what else transpired before saying something. I found a file back at the office on the property because my predecessors had been out there and detailed some of their accounts. There was even an opinion written several years ago by the Office of the Attorney General on the issue of the permit's expiration date. The opinion stated the permit was still valid, because it was issued before the law was amended to stipulate an expiration time period for permits. I also gathered that the marina was never completed because the site required extensive filling and dredging and they were going to do the work themselves. From what I saw it did not seem they had the proper equipment.

There was no additional action to take since technically he had a permit. However, the project description on the paperwork we had was so vague he could pretty much build whatever he wanted. I think the only opportunity through which the State could regain jurisdiction over the project site would be if the property was sold. If the buyer wanted to pursue the project, the permit would have to be transferred to them. There was one other way to have the project reviewed and we used it. He would need a Federal Permit under the Clean Water Act, so I notified the Army Corps of Engineers of the project. We thought they would probably give him a permit to build the marina but by getting them involved they could at least obtain a current plan.

I should point out that the goal of the State in protecting wetlands was not to prohibit construction of marinas, it just seeks to insure that they are built in the best location for navigational purposes and do not unnecessarily destroy wildlife habitat. Some shoreline areas would make a great site for a marina with minimum impacts while others result in major habitat destruction during construction.

DOCK IN A COASTAL WETLAND I

Having to conduct investigations in coastal areas did have the advantage of allowing me to explore remote and scenic areas as part of my job. One fall day, I received a call from a biologist with the Department of Marine Resources who said over the past several months he had noticed several new docks along Winnegance Bay and did not believe that their owners acquired permits. As the regional biologist, most wetland permits applications would be forwarded to him for review and comment so he would have remembered reviewing them. He could not really give me directions to each place because he had seen them from the water while doing his field work which included conducting shell fish surveys and other sampling. He offered to take me by boat to each site if I met him at his house.

Early one drizzly morning, a week or so later I drove up to meet him. His house was directly across from a public dock where he kept a sixteen foot aluminum boat with an outboard motor. We climbed in and took off. We began at the upper end of the inlet and had to cruise about twenty minutes to reach the area he was talking about. We quickly established a routine where I would photograph the suspect dock from the water, then he pulled up and I would get out and measure it. Next, I went to the house to see if anyone was home. Most of the docks seemed to serve summer cottages so typically no one was around. I tried to figure out what the addresses were so I could check the town records to identify the property owners. I did not have much success since there were no house numbers and the roads were often unmarked dirt tracks. One house was only accessible by water. We had been at it for a couple of hours when at the tenth, and last stop we came upon a brand new dock.

I photographed it and got out and measured it. This time when I went up to the house the owner was in fact home. Needless to say, he was surprised to have someone coming to his house from the water, much less a State official asking if he had a permit for the dock. I introduced myself and explained that I was investigating whether several docks in the area had been built with the proper permits. He stated that he recently bought the house and was renovating it; the previous owner told him there had been a dock there at one time and he should put one there. I explained that it was not that he could not build one, but as with other construction projects he needed a permit to do so. The State had an interest in insuring that it met certain standards, such as not interfering with navigation. Since it was not that big of a structure and was located on a rocky shoreline he should not have a problem getting the application approved, although I was not going to guarantee it because there could be an extenuating circumstance that I was not aware of. After getting his name and address I left him a copy of the law and an application. I also told him since it was a violation there was a possibility of us taking enforcement action and I would be in touch with him. To minimize confrontations, I usually stated it was not solely my decision whether or not to take action. I had to consult with my superiors and it was their determination as to the best means to achieve compliance with the law.

Upon consultation with my supervisor we decided to pursue formal enforcement action. We chose this course for several reasons: It was a strong case: the property owner told us when the dock was built and we determined a permit was not obtained. Deterrence: from the knowledge the state biologist provided it seemed that several structures in the area were constructed without permits. The publicity this case generated in the community would hopefully encourage people to find out what their responsibilities were and voluntarily come into compliance. Source of the complaint: since it came from a sister agency we wanted to do everything we could to demonstrate we valued their concern for the environment and enforcement of the law.

The homeowner filed a permit application in mid-December seeking after-the-fact approval for the dock. I forwarded a consent agreement after the holidays that required him to comply with any permit conditions if the application was approved, or in the event it was denied, he would agree to remove the structure. In addition, we assessed a penalty of four hundred dollars.

He waited until after he received his permit before signing the agreement and sending it back. It arrived at the beginning of April and was submitted for approval to the Board of Environmental Protection by the end of the month. After receiving the check for the penalty the case was closed. As a courtesy I sent the biologist who ferried me around a copy of the final agreement so he could see what happened.

I was never able to obtain enough information to verify if any of the other structures we examined that day were violations or not. Some of them may have been but it was not possible to prove. Basically, this guy got caught because he happened to be home at the time I showed up. With minor violations, whether someone was pursued is kind of like getting caught for speeding: a lot of people do it and get away with it; however, when you are stopped by that speed trap you will be prosecuted and fined.

DOCK IN A COASTAL WETLAND II

The following summer I had the opportunity to conduct a similar investigation. It also involved a complaint about the construction of a dock in a coastal wetland without a permit. The site was reported to be in the Town of Harpswell on Long Island which is located in the New Meadows River. To get a ride out there I contacted the Marine Patrol, which is a Division of the Department of Marine Resources. The Patrol's job is to enforce the State's fisheries laws. I was given the name and number of the officer whose territory the Island was in and instructed to call him directly.

I made an appointment to meet the officer in the parking lot of the Cooks Corner Shopping Center in Brunswick. From there, I followed him to where he kept his boat docked on the New Meadows River. The officer was a bit older than me, probably in his late twenties, he carried a gun and had the same training as a state trooper. He had a twenty five foot fiberglass speed boat with an engine that looked bigger than my car.

While casting off, we were talking and I thanked him again for taking the time to ferry me out to investigate the complaint. I figured he had something better to do. He said he was glad that I called because it gave him an excuse to get out on the water. He did not use the boat that much; he had such a large territory, he could not cover it quickly enough by water. It was more efficient for him to drive around to patrol the docks and examine a fisherman's catch as he unloaded it.

Little did I realize when we shoved off that he intended to do more than just ferry me around, he took full advantage of being out on the water to do some patrolling. Our destination was a thirty minute ride from where he kept his boat. After about ten minutes we saw a lobster boat coming toward us, as it came closer it made a sharp turn, pulling out of the main channel to go into a cove ahead of us. We suddenly sped up in pursuit. The officer decided to "pull him over" because he thought he may have gone in there to throw "short" lobsters overboard after recognizing the markings of the Patrol Boat. A short lobster is one that is below the legal size to capture. When you get a fishing license to catch lobsters they give you a brass measuring tool so you can determine if it is the legal size.

We hailed the boat, stopped it and pulled alongside. The officer asked for the lobsterman's license and gave it the once over. Then he measured the catch. The lobsterman only had about thirty lobsters and each one was legal so we thanked him for his time and went on our way. I am sure part of the reason the officer stopped him was the deterrent effect the fisherman's story would have. He would be sure to tell his buddies that the Marine Patrol is out and about making everyone think twice about keeping short lobsters.

As we went on our way nothing eventful happened for at least ten minutes; until we came upon three lobster boxes tied to a buoy. A lobster box is a wooden crate that floats and that is used by fishermen to keep their catch fresh. The officer wanted to check to see if there were any short lobsters in them as well. We had already looked in one, it was empty, and we're idling up to another when someone on shore started yelling for us to get away from the buoy. We were about a hundred yards from shore. The officer stared at this guy for a few seconds and without saying a word kicks the boat into gear and speeds toward shore at full throttle. As we're heading straight toward the rocks (there was no dock), he turns to me and says that when we get next to shore we both will jump out. It will be my job to hold the boat. When the guy onshore sees us coming at him at full speed he turns and runs away. As we approached the rocks we had to slow down to find a spot to land so the guy had a good head start. We both jumped at the same time, the officer handed me a line to the boat and took off after the guy. I waited and made sure the boat did not hit the rocks. After about fifteen minutes the officer came back and said it was a false alarm. The guy ran up to his house and was calling the Marine Patrol: he thought he caught someone stealing his buoy and crates and they were coming to get him.

Needless to say my investigation was fairly boring compared to his. We found the Island which was a couple of acres of pine covered granite with two cabins on it. One was brand new; it looked like one of those kits you put together yourself, the other was an older looking cottage. Each one had a new dock in front of it. We tied up at one and got out. I took some pictures, recorded their sizes, and noted the characteristics of the shoreline. We had an uneventful cruise back to the mainland.

I was able to identify the property owners from the land records at the town office since I knew the name of the Island and there were only two structures on the whole thing. I first contacted the owner of the older looking place who maintained he had replaced an existing dock that had been there for years. I had no way to prove otherwise. I dropped the case because the law did not regulate the replacement of existing structures. The owner of the new cabin admitted to having built a new structure and agreed to file an after-the-fact application for a permit.

In contrast to the previous case we chose not to pursue formal enforcement action this time. The reason for handling these cases differently was that, subsequent to the resolution of the former one, the State instituted significantly higher fees for after-the-fact applications for minor projects such as this. Therefore, the regulations automatically penalized those who did not get their permits up front. These cases essentially had the same result while the new regulations freed me to spend my time developing agreements for more egregious violations with larger impacts.

THE PISCATAQUA RIVER

The office received a tip from the code enforcement officer (CEO) in the town of Eliot, that a stream and coastal wetland were filled in to build a house. Eliot is a small town at the southern tip of Maine that borders the Piscataqua River. A CEO is the local official responsible for issuing permits and enforcing the local building codes and land use ordinances. Several of the CEOs I ran across were conscientious about keeping us informed of projects they thought the State may have jurisdiction over. While it is nice to think you have their respect so that they will confide in you, sometimes I thought I was contacted in the hope I would come in and resolve an unpleasant situation so they did not have to. In many ways the CEO's job could be very political: if competency in their pursuit of compliance was perceived to be overzealous they could be out of a job.

On a crisp October morning, I met the CEO at the town office. I drove us over to the site in my car. The property was only a short drive from his office. On the way over he explained he called our office because he was concerned about the activity he saw on the property when he went out to conduct a routine inspection of the contractor's work on the house construction. I followed his directions to a pleasantly wooded driveway that opened to a huge Komatsu backhoe. Next to that was a brand new cedar sided house; the lawn had not even been planted yet. I knocked on the door to see if anyone was home. There was no answer.

At the front of the house the CEO showed me the swale that he thought might be considered a stream. It was a channel of sorts. It was dry and did not have a mineral bottom except for some excess gravel that was pushed into it from the driveway. I did not consider it to be either a stream or a violation. The back side of the house, next to the River, was a different story.

There was a great view of the Piscataqua River because all of the trees on the embankment had been cut down. At the base of the embankment was a wetland area that extended out for a couple of hundred feet until it met the open water. At this time of year, most of the plants were brown and withered but it was obviously a wetland. This stretch of the River was influenced by the tide and the plants looked to be salt tolerant species indicative of a coastal wetland.

At the foot of the embankment, a u-shaped dike had been constructed to form a shallow pond. The dike was about three feet high, five feet wide, forming a basin of about 10,000 square feet. Both arms of the "U" met at the base of the embankment which was about twenty five feet high. Most of the area enclosed by the dike had been excavated. See Figure 3 for site drawing.

We climbed down to get a closer look. Behind the dike, a large hole had been dug which had filled with water. The steel gray marine clay that was dredged out of the hole was placed on top of the wetland plants. The backhoe in the front yard must have been used to do this work. You could see where the machine's treads tore up the vegetation and turned over the earth when it had run back and forth. I was rather surprised to actually see a wetland torn up like this. Most calls of such activity usually turned out to be some activity near the wetland, not actually in it.

The dike looked as if it had been built many years before: it was over grown with grass and weeds, there was even the remains of an old rotted flood gate. Since the dike was there, I wanted to

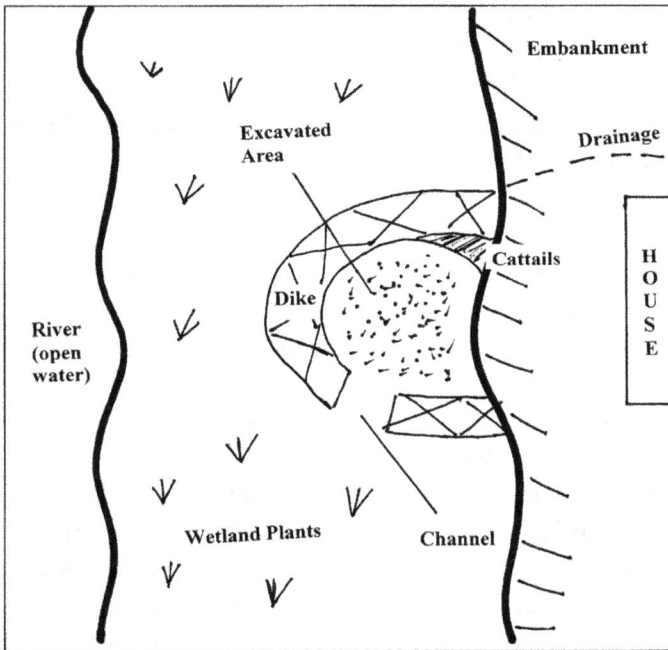

Figure 3 – Piscataqua River Wetland Site

be sure there would be no doubt it was a coastal wetland under the State's jurisdiction. Criteria for jurisdiction included the presence of specific salt tolerant plants or whether the area was washed by the tide. Although the State only had jurisdiction over fresh water wetlands ten or more acres in size, there was no minimum size limit on coastal wetlands.

I recognized the salt tolerant plant spartina patens, which is indicative of marine environments, to be growing in the affected area. It also looked as if the tide washed over the area through breeches in the dike. However, at the foot of the embankment were some cattails, which are indicative of freshwater wetlands. These eventually gave way to the shorter marine grasses.

This appeared to be such a flagrant violation I wanted to be certain there could not be a challenge to the State's jurisdiction. My concern was that an argument could be made the affected area was a small freshwater wetland that was separated from the coastal wetland and the River by the dike. It may not have been a good argument from a natural resources stand point, but to build a strong case you have to anticipate what a violator will try and use as a defense. I planned on getting an expert to verify my observations and support my case.

Before I left, I completed my documentation of the site by measuring the size of the affected area with a tape measure and taking several pictures. In all, approximately six thousand square feet had been excavated, filled and torn up.

The next day, I called the property owner, introduced myself, and told him I had been out to his house by the River in response to a complaint. I explained that the excavation in the wetland was a violation of State law and he could be subject to an enforcement action. We agreed to meet at the property the following week to discuss the violation and how it could be resolved. Prior to going to the site, I met the CEO at his office. This time we went over in separate cars. He explained that he wanted to make it clear that the State was acting independently of the town in this matter. While he supported our action, he did not want to be identified as taking the initiative. That left it to me to be the bad guy.

When discussing violations and enforcement actions with violators there are a few broad categories of behavior: in denial ("I did not do anything wrong. The law does not apply to me because...''); deflect attention ("What about what so and so did?"); or friendly and cooperative ("Sorry I didn't know, it was an accident, how can I fix it?''). This property owner was a doctor who was the latter; however, their outward demeanor is not always indicative of how cooperative they will be.

I introduced myself and began explaining "The CEO had called me because he thought State permits may be necessary for the work you're doing. Upon inspecting the property it appeared to me that you needed one." He said "Oh is that all, how do I get it?" He wanted to finish digging out the area behind the dike to create a pond. I also asked him who the contractor was that did the work for him. He gave me the name of an outfit from New Hampshire. I then went back to the issue of the permit and explained "We have a problem. To obtain a coastal wetlands permit you must demonstrate that the project does not have unreasonable impacts on wildlife habitat, water flow, and a number of other criteria. It looks to me like you're destroying the wetland and in my opinion an application will be denied. You have every right to go ahead and apply, but I think you could save yourself the trouble. I suggest the area be restored as soon as possible."

At this point, he went with the "are you sure you have jurisdiction" argument. He did not think it was a coastal wetland because the dike separated the area where he was digging from the rest of the wetland. We walked down to the dike to get a closer look. I explained it is a coastal wetland because of the type of plants that are present. He asked which ones. I got down on my hands and knees to point out seaside golden rod and spartina patens which are species tolerant of salt water that we used to identify coastal wetlands. I also pointed out the gaps in the dike where water could flow through when the tide came in.

He still wanted to complete the pond and explore the option of getting a permit. I gave him a pamphlet that described the law and permit application procedures. I stated again he was free to apply but not to be surprised if the application was denied. In addition, the Department would be reviewing his case to determine if formal enforcement action is warranted. This could include penalties which are a minimum of one hundred dollars per day of violation.

I would have to consult my superiors and notify him what course of action we would pursue. This was the last time we met.

My next step was to get an expert on wetlands plants out there to verify my facts. Once again I relied upon a regional biologist from the Department of Marine Resources. His opinion would be doubly valuable: in addition to delineating the wetland, part of his job was to review coastal wetland permit applications and provide comments on a project's anticipated impacts. Frequently, it was their recommendation that led to a project's approval or denial. If he agreed with my findings at this early stage of the case, I hoped to use his opinion to convince the doctor not to file an application, as well as, eliminate the permit review process from providing an excuse for the doctor to delay settling the case.

For the third week in a row, I found myself out inspecting the same property. The biologist's first impression of the site was that some enterprising hunters probably built the dike to form a small pond to create open water to lure ducks to the shore. The hunters could take cover in the woods instead of having to sit out on the marsh. The biologist agreed with my assessment that the area the doctor wished to excavate was a coastal wetland as identified by the various indicator species that I recognized plus a few others. In addition, the cattails that were present were a narrow leaf variety that are tolerant of brackish water. Since the coastal wetland is contiguous with the brackish area, and cannot be separated, the whole wetland area behind the dike was under State jurisdiction. He also agreed that there would be little chance for approval of an application to dredge this site, especially with the amount of open water available in the form of the River. The biologist even offered to provide technical advice to restore the disturbed area.

It didn't take us very long to decide to prosecute this one. It was the most egregious violation of a coastal wetland I had seen. My supervisor readily agreed when I showed him the pictures. The following week I wrote a letter to the doctor summarizing the findings from my site visits, suggested that he restore the site as soon as possible, and informed him we would be proceeding with a consent agreement. At this time I also called the contractor to inform him of the violation.

The contractors were two brothers from New Hampshire and said they were not familiar with the Maine Laws. They were hired to put in the septic system and said the doctor asked them to do the pond since they had the backhoe on site. They had recently purchased the piece of equipment and needed the practice with it so decided to give it a try.

By the end of January, I had drafted and forwarded a consent agreement naming the contractor and doctor as codefendants. It required the payment of a six thousand dollar penalty and restoration of the affected area. If there was more than one party involved in an alleged violation I would name both in one agreement and let them work out who paid the penalty or conducted the restoration. This only works if both parties are willing to cooperate with each other. If they do not, I must negotiate separately with each one.

Instead of the doctor responding, I received a call from his attorney. This lawyer impressed me less than most. His office was in New Hampshire and it was evident he was not well versed with the Maine statutes that applied to his client's case. He kept on asking basic questions about the law's jurisdiction and applicability to the activities in question. I ended up sending him a pamphlet that outlined everything. He responded with the usual feeble arguments that his client did not know a permit was necessary. You could make that argument yourself. If you're going to pay a lawyer they should challenge your case on points of constitutional law, evidence, or jurisdiction. I agreed to reconsider the provisions of the consent agreement and would contact him.

In mid-March, I forwarded a revised agreement. In response to his tough negotiating style and insightful arguments on the merits of the case, I slightly lowered the penalty and gave them more time to restore the site. In the cover letter I expressed the Department's willingness to entertain an application if they wanted to file one. However, I also stressed that if they kept on stalling I would have no choice but to file an action in court. I never received a reply from either party. In April, I began preparations for going to court.

We had such a strong case that we decided to file a complaint in court using our "80K authority.[6]" This rule established what is known as a summary procedure, which means that the violator can answer the complaint orally in court rather than in writing. Even though I was not a lawyer, the Rule allowed authorized representatives to present the case to the Court on behalf of the State. I would in essence act as the prosecuting attorney: presenting the State's case, explaining the law, its application, our evidence, and call witnesses. The benefit of the procedure is that it provides a quicker, less formal, and less expensive system for the prosecution of people who violate land use laws without sacrificing their due process rights.

The first step is to write a document known as a citation and complaint. This document describes the facts of the alleged violation and summarizes the relevant statutes. It is filed with the District Court in conjunction with getting a date for the trial. This document tells the judge what the issues before the court are and what actions are requested for him to order. In this case, we asked him to order restoration of the wetland and assess a six thousand dollar penalty.

A lawyer with the Attorney General's Office provided guidance on drafting the complaint. By the time I was able to draft it and get approval from our superiors it was already August. The reason why it took so long was that I also had to construct the case to make sure we could prove what we described in the complaint. (Meanwhile, I was still handling a full caseload and conducting investigations of new complaints.) I had to be able to prove to the judge that the doctor owned the property , the excavation took place, and this activity occurred in a coastal wetland. As evidence, I had the pictures I took, as well as, my own testimony and that of witnesses. I planned to call the CEO and the biologist.

While making my preparations I went to the registry of deeds to make sure I correctly cited the property and that the doctor was the sole owner. He was, but I noted the bank held a mortgage and someone else filed a lien. As parties with an interest in the property I forwarded a letter notifying them of the impending court action. The individual with the lien called me to say he was the contractor who built the house and claimed the doctor still owed him money. The doctor asked him if he would excavate the wetland. He said no. He told the doctor he might need a permit to do something like that and suggested he contact the State to find out. He offered to be a witness against the doctor and testify that they had this conversation.

The sheriff served summonses to the defendants with a copy of the complaint that required them to appear in court to respond to the charges. The court date was set for early October, a year after I first documented the violation.

The week before the trial I visited the site with the CEO and the biologist. It had been almost a year since we were last there and I felt it would help our testimony if we had the site fresh in our minds. I discussed our testimony and reviewed the types of questions I would ask. I especially wanted the biologist to be able to clearly characterize the types of plants to identify the coastal wetland and summarize the impacts of the work. I also wanted to see the condition for the site. For all I knew he may have restored it.

As the day of the trial approached I was ready to go to court. I had plenty of evidence and good witnesses. Since this was my first court appearance I will admit I was extremely nervous. An Assistant Attorney General was supposed to accompany me for legal and moral support but she called the day before to bail out on me: "A case I'm handling exploded. I won't be there. Good luck." District Court is supposed to be informal so I figured I would be alright. The morning of the hearing, a few minutes before I was going to leave, the doctor's lawyer called to ask for a continuance. This is a request for a postponement to allow additional time for negotiations. As a matter of courtesy I agreed and called the court to let them know that we did not need the hearing scheduled today as we were going to continue trying to settle the complaint out-of-court. At the time, I did not think to reschedule an alternative date because I figured I had the defendant's attention now. By early November, I had redrafted the consent agreement and forwarded it once again.

The summons was enough to get the contractor's cooperation. The contractor responded by saying he wanted to go out to the property and restore the wetland but the doctor would not allow it. It did not sound like they were cooperating with each other so I offered to negotiate separately with him. I was hoping if I could reach a settlement with the contractor I could use that as leverage against the doctor. It took another week of negotiation back and forth but I finally got the contractor to agree to pay a two thousand dollar penalty. I made an appointment to meet with him at his office to get a signature on the agreement.

Usually, when you're going to have any kind of settlement conference it is better to have the defendant come to you. This way you gain the advantage of having them on unfamiliar territory. However, I wanted to get a signature as soon as possible so I took an agreement to their office in New Hampshire and had them sign it. Were they ever mad. Not at me, but at the doctor. After all this mess he got them into he still had not paid their bill. At this time, they volunteered to testify against the doctor that they excavated the area at his request. I felt sorry for having to put them through all this. They had just taken the business over from their Dad; however, I had no choice as it was the most blatant violation of the coastal wetlands act I had ever seen. I do believe that if they knew better they would not have done it. Anyway, they said they were going to stick to business in New Hampshire for now on. Since they were summoned to appear before the court I said I might have them testify.

The doctor still refused to settle. During my next conversation with his attorney I mentioned that the contractor signed an agreement. This undermined their defense because the contractor admitted to violating the coastal wetlands act on the doctor's property. If they stuck together they might have put up a better defense. A week later they agreed to sign a consent agreement. However, we still had to negotiate acceptable terms.

The following week, the doctor's attorney called me. He began trying to convince me that the "pond" was not under state jurisdiction because the dike was built thirty years ago: before the existence of the coastal wetlands act. I told him that did not matter as it was still a coastal wetland as indicated by the plants and the gaps in the dike that let the tide flow in. He then got around to arguing that the State trampled his client's constitutional rights by "taking" the property without just compensation by denying the doctor his pond. I countered by citing the decision in the Hall Case where the Maine Supreme Court found the regulation of the property under the coastal wetlands act did not violate the owner's rights if they still had some use of it. It did not have to be the highest and best use, just some significant use. Besides, here we were talking about only a small percentage of the total lot that was regulated as a coastal wetland. The doctor was able to build his house; cut down a number of trees; and enjoy unrestricted use of the overwhelming majority of the property. I finished with the fact that the violation had been in existence for a year and if we sought the statutory minimum one hundred dollars per day of violation, the fine could be in the tens of thousands of dollars. He ended by saying he wanted to consult with his client.

In early December, I forwarded another revised agreement for him to review. The first of the year came with still no response. I tried several times to reach the attorney on the phone. He would no longer accept my phone calls. I decided to set another court date. I forwarded another letter notifying the lawyer the hearing was rescheduled for the first Monday in February. The Thursday before the trial he finally called asking for another continuance. I said "No way, we are going to court unless I have a signed agreement by the close of business tomorrow." He agreed.

I drove down in a snow storm to pick up the agreement at his office in New Hampshire and filed it with the court that afternoon. The lawyer did not even take the time to speak to me, he just left the agreement with his secretary. When I called the biologist and the CEO to tell them they did not have to go to court on Monday they were pleasantly surprised that the case was settled with the stipulation that the coastal wetland area be restored. I got a two thousand dollar penalty out of him too.

Once the contractor paid his fine, that was the end of our case against him. The agreement with the doctor gave him a month to pay the penalty. As for restoring the wetland, since it was the middle of winter I outlined a schedule with milestone dates throughout the spring and summer when he should accomplish tasks such as filling in the hole, leveling the site, and replanting vegetation. It is important to check to make sure these activities are completed but I had to pass that responsibility on to someone else. I changed jobs within the Department and my caseload was distributed to my colleagues.

This case demonstrates the value and necessity of being able to pursue actions in court. At several points in the negotiations the violator appeared to be cooperative and responsive to my requests. However, he didn't follow through until his only choice was to explain things to a judge.

CHAPTER 6

COASTAL SAND DUNE SYSTEMS

Coastal sand dunes are sand deposits within a marine beach system above high tide including, but not limited to, beach berms, frontal dune ridges, back dune areas, and other sand areas deposited by wave or wind action. Coastal sand dunes may extend into coastal wetlands. It is often due to the existence of a dune barrier system that the area shoreward of it is protected from ocean storms and a coastal wetland is able to form behind it.

Waves are the most important force in beach formation since they not only carry sand shoreward but are also subsequently involved in most of the daily and long-term beach processes. Waves are formed by winds, either locally or far offshore. Waves can erode or build up beaches, depending on factors such as wave speed or direction, and the shape of the sea floor. Storms occur only for brief periods of time throughout annual cycles of beach processes, but they are the most important control in cycles of erosion and accretion.

Dunes are the most fragile zone of the beach complex. Sand is only held there by the few plants that can survive the dry, harsh conditions. These plants form the frontline in a succession of plants that act as pioneers into the new and unstable territory of the sand beach.

Coastal sand dune plants have specialized life cycle features which enable them to survive in an extremely hostile environment. They tolerate stresses such as salt spray, sand burial, and sand removal, as well as extreme changes in soil moisture, air moisture, and soil chemistry. American beach grass is a dominant perennial plant of young active dunes, especially the front ridge. Here the sand shifts rapidly, and beach grass has adapted so that it can survive up to one meter of sand burial by rapidly extending rhizomes. Its position on the front ridge traps sand and helps stabilize the dunes so other species can come in.

Sand beaches exist in a dynamic equilibrium, responding to storms or a rise in sea levels by slowly migrating – retreating toward the land. The form and position of beach and dune features respond to even the slight changes in wind, waves, and storms. When people interrupt this movement by compacting and confining sand with roads and buildings, and further disrupt the flow of sand with jetties and seawalls, they interfere with the natural processes that maintain the beaches and assure their destruction.

Recognizing the dynamic and fragile nature of sand dune systems, the State required permits for construction in these areas.[7] The types of structures that require permits include seawalls which are built parallel to the shoreline. Constructed of wood or stone, they are designed to withstand wave impact during high tides or storms. However, their construction typically harms the dune system. This damage can occur over a short or long period of time. The steepened profile created by a wall reflects the storm wave energy striking the shoreline which in turn increases erosion. It also increases the intensity of long shore currents, hastening removal of the beach and acts as a barrier preventing the exchange of sand between dunes and beach. Finally, it concentrates wave energy and current energy at the ends of the wall, increasing erosion at these points. For this reason, your seawall, while protecting your property may adversely impact your neighbors.

CAMP ELLIS

Over time, rivers delivered large quantities of sand from glacial deposits in the mountains that eventually flowed to the coast and formed beaches. Dams were erected on the Saco River during the eighteenth and nineteenth centuries and had the capacity to trap large quantities of sand that would have become beach material. In the late nineteenth century, the U.S. Army Corps of Engineers built rock jetties at the mouth of the River to promote safe navigation. They removed (dredged) an enormous sand bar at the mouth of the River. This material was added to the land at Camp Ellis (extending it seven hundred feet seaward) and built upon. The new land was not being replenished by receiving additional sand from the River. The long jetties at the mouth of the River trapped the sand that led to channel shoaling. This in turn deprived adjacent Camp Ellis of sand and led to severe erosion there. Finally, seawalls have reflected wave energy and also prevented sand from moving onto the beach.

Around Labor Day, I received a call from a gentleman who had just purchased a waterfront cottage. This "new" waterfront property owner contacted the office to determine what his responsibilities were prior to undertaking construction activities in the dune system. I made an appointment to meet him at his house on Eastern Avenue. This was a road that ran parallel to the water. The only thing between the house and the open water was a wooden seawall made of two by tens standing on end with some large boulders strewn around at its base.

The owner explained that he and his wife had just bought the place with another couple and they wanted to know what work they could do without permits and what would require one. The house looked poorly maintained, a real fixer upper. Even so, due to its waterfront location the only way they could afford it was to share the expenses with friends.

First, I determined that they were definitely on the dune system, and second, part of the property was a coastal wetland. They wanted to know if they could reinforce the seawall and raise the house. Permits would be required to do both. I doubted the seawall expansion would be approved because it had the potential to exacerbate erosion at the beach, but raising the house would probably be approved so long as it remained on piers which would allow flood waters to flow unimpeded underneath it. Finally, he inquired if he could bring fill in to level off the lot. That would require a permit too.

The next time I heard from him was in January, after a nor'easter tore along the coast. The heavy surf combined with high tides destroyed his seawall. He wanted information on repairing it. Again, I met him at the site. The property looked totally different: about half the boards in the seawall had been washed away, those remaining moved back and forth with the tide like blades of grass. The driveway, and most of the yard, was gone and the septic tank was exposed and broken. The first time I was there, there was just a crawl space under the house, now you could park a truck underneath it. The only reason the house still stood was that it was built on poles and the water flowed between them like the pilings that support a dock.

I informed him that he could replace the wall with one of similar size and dimensions without a permit. I also recommended he apply for an emergency permit to place fill under the house. They were lucky that this was the last big storm of the season to cause much erosion. Early in the spring, I revisited the property. They had placed fill under the house and repaired the driveway. The material was obtained from the excavations from the sewer project discussed in the preceding chapter. By the end of the summer they had replaced the seawall too. However, after owning the house for a year, they had spent considerable time and money to make sure it did not wash away, never mind fixing it up and enjoying it.

I felt sorry for these people but they were fighting a losing battle. After a year they decided to just try and cut their losses. They stretched themselves financially to buy the cottage, had not even enjoyed one summer in it, and put it up for sale to try and recoup their investment. They also told me they were going to try and sue the realtor for not disclosing to them that the property was subject to severe erosion.

CHAPTER 7

RESOURCE EXTRACTION ACTIVITIES

As illustrated by the previous chapters, laws can be structured to regulate specific types of ecologic systems: rivers, streams, lakes, ponds, and freshwater and coastal wetlands. In addition, laws can also be structured to control the location and scope of large developments that due to their sheer size or purpose may substantially affect the local environment. One example of such a project is strip mines for sand and gravel.

Sand and gravel are important materials that are needed for most types of construction projects and in some cases in very large quantities as in the construction of roads. Due to the large volumes that may be necessary it is highly desirable to find a source close to your project in order to minimize transportation costs. Thus, proximity to projects can drive the development of these resources in nearby areas.

Concerns associated with the strip mines arise from large areas being cleared of vegetation which increases the potential for erosion. Sand and gravel deposits can also be associated with drinking water aquifers as well as recharge areas for groundwater. So the manner in which the area is excavated can impact these water resources. The property must also be properly surveyed and reasonable buffers maintained to minimize impacts to adjacent landowners. If you were the neighbor, you would not want the adjacent property owner digging up and selling your land or be left with a steep drop on the property line. I have seen some abandoned operations with sand cliffs seventy five feet high. Someone could either fall or the material could collapse on top of them. A plan is also necessary for reclaiming the site once it is played out or no longer needed. Regulating the excavation of material may seem like an infringement on private property rights, but it was only insofar as necessary to protect public safety, adjacent property owners from impacts, and public water resources.

State jurisdiction of the law which regulated resource extraction activities of this type was triggered if you opened a new one, or expanded an old one, by more than five acres. You could dig to the center of the earth if you wanted to if the affected area was less than five acres, but if you went beyond that the whole site fell under State jurisdiction.

BENNET ROAD SITE

In the early spring, I received an anonymous complaint of a strip mine having been expanded by more than five acres without the appropriate permits. The operation was reported to be on the Bennet Road in New Gloucester. I drove out to the site to see what was going on. I located the Bennet Road and the mine activity with little difficulty.

As I drove up the road I came upon a sand desert that had been denuded of all vegetation. This was the strip mine. One edge of it ran parallel to the road. Using the car's odometer I measured it to be approximately one quarter of a mile long. The width appeared to vary from one hundred to two hundred yards. The site was very active with front loaders digging and trucks hauling sand and gravel away. As I passed the gate I noted the company's name on the machinery. My initial field inspection was complete. I did not even get out of the car; this was what we call a windshield in-spection. What I knew so far was that there was a big hole in the ground. What I had to figure out is how big it was and when did it get that way.

The reason I did not bother approaching the operator at this time is that they could either already have a permit, or more likely, the site may be exempt from State regulation. I could just ask them, but the typical answers were: "I don't know." or "It's been here for as long as anyone can remember." Before contacting anyone I liked to gather as much information on these types of sites as was avail-able. Now that I had the exact location of the property and the name of the operator it would be easy to check if a permit had been issued.

I checked our files and learned that no permits were issued for any strip mines in all of New Gloucester. Not many rural commu-nities required local permits and New Gloucester was no exception. A call to the Town Hall confirmed they did not have any records on the site either. A good source of historical records for determin-ing large scale land use activities over a period of many years was the county office of the Soil Conservation Service (SCS). Part of the SCS mission is to identify and map the various soil types throughout their jurisdictions to be used as a land use planning tool; primarily for agriculture. The SCS publishes surveys that have the soil types superimposed on aerial photographs. In addition to the published surveys they also have the original photos. These photographs provide a record of the land use activities during that time period. I went to the Cumberland County Office to see what was available. They had two sets of pictures of the affected area that were taken six years apart.

I located the appropriate quadrants, and was able to pin-point the strip mine from the adjoining roads. A comparison of the photos indicated a difference in size between the before and after pictures.

Knowing the scale of the photos, I was able to calculate the size of the affected area in acres. The difference in size of the operation, as shown by the two photographs, would tell me how much the active area expanded between the times when the pictures were taken. This difference turned out to be nine acres. See Figure 4. I did not determine the difference that may have occurred after that, but it did not really matter since the whole area now came under our jurisdiction.

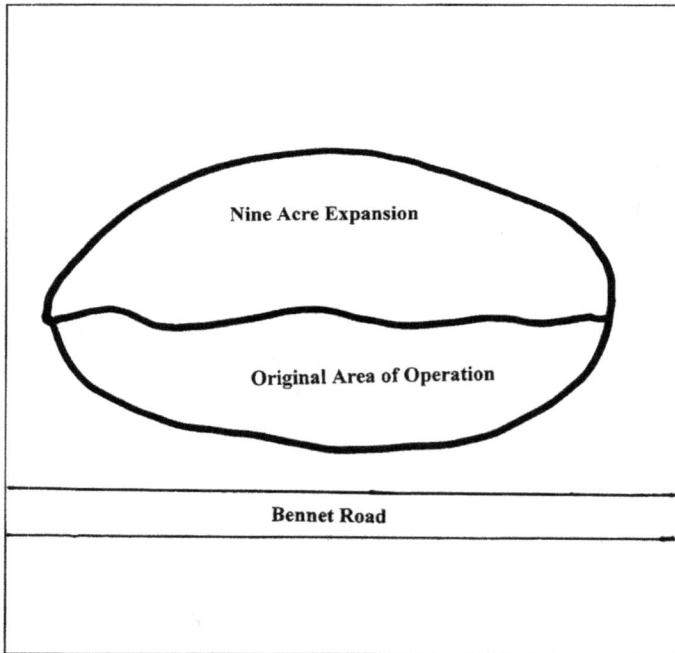

Figure 4 – Bennet Road Resource Extraction Site

Due to a lack of consistently good records on these types of activities it was often difficult to prove a violation or to assert the State's jurisdiction. A picture is worth a thousand words: This time we had good documentation of the violation and decided to pursue formal enforcement action.

The company operating the site was one of the largest heavy construction contractors in the State. I called the company and asked to speak with whoever was in charge of their operation in New Gloucester. I was transferred to one of the vice-presidents. After introducing myself, I explained that I had been investigating the Bennet Road site in response to a complaint and had documentation of a violation of State law. I confirmed that their company was indeed the operator but they did not own the property. He informed me that they had leased the right to excavate sand and gravel from the site for nearly twenty years. I concluded our conversation by stating that they should file an after-the-fact permit application, suspend operations at the site until they receive a permit, and that I would be drafting a consent agreement to resolve the violation. I forwarded a letter summarizing my investigation and our conversation.

After digesting some of this information they responded by arguing that the borrow pit was exempt from regulation because the material currently being excavated was for a State Turnpike Authority project. I called their contact at the Authority and explained the background of the case. They stated the Authority contracts out all large construction projects and they do not assume any responsibility or shield the companies from applicable State laws. After neutralizing their main challenge they were fairly cooperative and filed a permit application in June.

It took six months for the consent agreement to be reviewed by the Attorney General's Office. I didn't get a draft to the violators until mid-winter. The agreement assessed a penalty of seven thousand five hundred dollars. They felt it was too much money considering all they had to go through: filing the permit application and not being able to use the site unless and until it was approved. They didn't want to pay anything. I got them to agree to a fifty five hundred dollar penalty by showing them an agreement for a similar violation with a similar penalty that I recently settled with one of their chief competitors. They accepted the argument that similar violations deserved similar penalties. The agreement was signed in April, about a year after I first discovered the violation. The most important aspect of this settlement was actually getting the site under a permit which would address how it would be reclaimed and revegetated after they were finished.

ELIOT SITE

Approximately a year and a half before I started working for the Department, the office received a complaint about a strip mine operating without a permit. A few months after I began work, the investigator who had the case took another job in the Department and the case was assigned to me.

The file on the case did not contain much evidence that was very useful other than the location of the site. I basically had to start the investigation from scratch. In November, I was finally able to visit the property which was in the Town of Eliot. There was a large borrow pit for sand and gravel several acres in size that was formed by cutting away at a large hill. There were very steep vertical slopes at least fifty feet high. The hill was probably formed from a glacial outwash deposit.

My next stop was the Soil Conservation Service Office to compare aerial photographs of the site to see if the excavated area had been expanded beyond the allowable limits without a permit. The first set of pictures proved the active area of the borrow pit to be approximately four and a half acres in size. Pictures taken five years later, showed it to be approximately 18 acres. See Figure 5. A check of the Department's records indicated that the operation was in violation because a permit for this expansion had not been obtained.

The following day I called the code enforcement officer to determine who the property owner was. He gave me the name and said the operation was situated on a ninety acre parcel of land. He said he did not know anything else about the history of the site.

I was not able to contact the property owner until late January. During a phone conversation he indicated that approximately one third of the borrow pit was on his property and the other two thirds on the abutting lot owned by someone else.

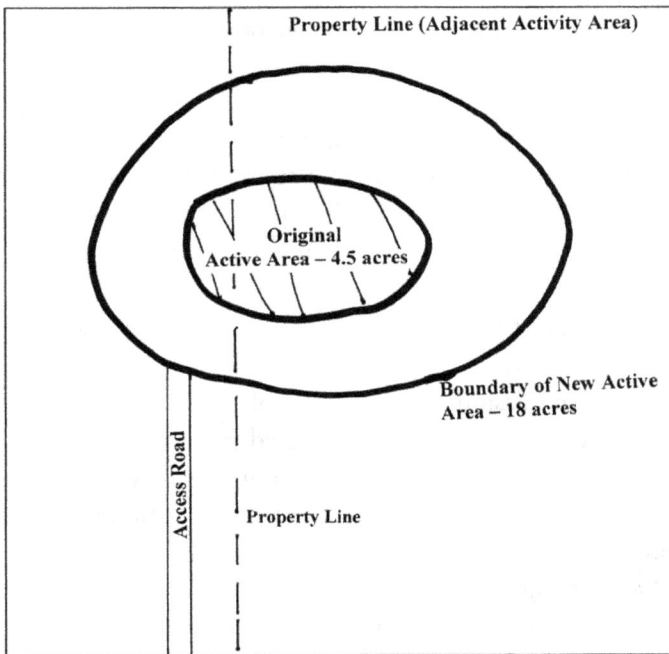

Figure 5 – Eliot Resource Extraction site

He also explained that neither he nor the other property owner did the actual digging. That was handled by a third party, who was a contractor, who paid them for what he took and used the material in his various construction projects. Although it was not entirely on his property, I informed him, for purposes of the law, the operation was considered a single project and all three of them were equally responsible for violating State land use laws.

I called these other two parties and told them about my investigation. The contractor complained about being singled out: there were numerous other similar operations in the area that he felt should be scrutinized. I told him to forward information about their locations and we would investigate them too.

We decided to pursue a consent agreement because we had a good case and it was in a portion of the State that would benefit from the attendant publicity due to the rapid expansion and development of similar operations.

I followed the phone calls with a letter to each party explaining my investigation, the violation, and the Department's intention to pursue a consent agreement. I also requested that they file an after-the-fact application to obtain a permit to bring the site into compliance. I asked them to submit the application within fifty days.

In response, the contractor called his state representative to complain about this "unfair" treatment. The representative contacted the Commissioner's office. He told the Commissioner how his constituent felt he was being singled out and described three other nearby operations that should be investigated. In addition, he raised the subject of mitigating factors such as the material from the site being used to complete projects under contracts for the State Department of Transportation. Such communication always complicates the handling of a case because of the legislator's role in determining the Department's annual budget. On the one hand, you have a responsibility to uphold the laws of the State; however, in doing so you do not want to alienate someone who has tremendous power over the Department. Nevertheless, you also do not want to succumb to any political pressure that would allow someone who broke the law to get away with it because of who they know. It is difficult to be sensitive to the representatives concerns and not appear to all interested parties to be unduly influenced by them.

I, in turn, received instructions from my superiors to grant the contractor more time to submit an application and report back to him on the other operations. It turned out that the sites he described had already been investigated by my colleagues and all were currently in compliance with the law. I called the contractor and gave him until mid-August to get the application in, which would be six months after my original request. We did not really care whether it was two or six months, we just wanted to set some type of milestones to work towards other that "get it in when you can." I also told him that the other sites he described were in compliance, but that we were open to investigating any other potential violations. These conversations were again documented by follow up correspondence. However, we did not think it was a good indicator of his future cooperation that he went straight to his legislator for an extension instead of contacting us directly. We feared he would take this route again since it appeared to him to be very successful in getting an extension.

A few months later, at the beginning of the summer, the contractor contacted me indicating that the landowners would prefer to submit a plan to close the site instead of obtaining a permit for its continued operation. I said that was fine and the plan developed would be incorporated into the consent agreement.

After consulting with our technical staff, I requested that the plan should include the following elements: contoured site drawings illustrating the existing topography and another set showing how it would be after the site was graded. The plans should also illustrate roads, streams, wet areas, and property lines, an erosion control plan, including the type of vegetation to be established; and a work schedule for regrading and revegetation.

While this was going on, I received another complaint about the contractor disposing of tree stumps from a road building project on property off Hanscom Road, again in Eliot. In May, I inspected the site and determined that approximately twenty stumps had been put in a small freshwater wetland. This waste was disposed of in such a manner that groundwater could be contaminated beyond the solid waste boundary, in violation of the waste management rules. Since it was not that big of a mess yet, I just fired off a letter telling him to stop and not dispose of any more materials at the site. I hoped that this would demonstrate that, when the circumstances warranted it, we would exercise appropriate discretion in regard to the enforcement of the law.

August came with the deadline for submission of the closing plan. I received a call from the contractor stating that the consultant drafting the plan would need another six to eight weeks to complete it. The assistant attorney general working on the case with me suggested raising the proposed fine in the consent agreement for the delay in attempting to come into compliance. At the end of August, we forwarded a draft consent agreement to the three parties that stipulated for them to submit a closing plan for the site and assessed a penalty of six thousand dollars. The one agreement named all three parties so they could work out amongst themselves who would do what. They would all be jointly responsible for complying with the terms of the agreement.

I heard from the contractor fairly quickly. After stating that he thought the fine was too high, he wanted to know who complained. When I told him I did not know; he threatened to go over my head and again went into how he was being singled out. I responded how we reviewed the other cases he described earlier and that we determined the State did not have any jurisdiction. In addition, the fine we were seeking was approximately the same amount we assessed in a similar case. Besides, six thousand dollars was a bargain considering the site was in violation for several years. In addition, he would be avoiding the five hundred dollar permit fee by submitting a closing plan instead. Although he denied it, he must have realized some economic benefit from the operation over the years. He also expressed frustration since he was not the landowner he did not have the option to apply for a permit. I did not have any control over that either, and in order not to seem unreasonable, I told him I would reconsider his position and discuss it with our attorneys.

The next day, one of the landowners called. He did not want to sign either. He said he was not responsible and did not have the money for the penalty. I responded that it was his land, he gave the contractor permission to excavate, and he had made some money off the site over the years. He said he never made much. I was rather skeptical of this argument. Why would they operate a borrow pit for so many years and remove so much material at no small expense, if they all lost money year in and year out. I suggested that he consult with the contractor on the terms of the agreement because it was written so you can work out who will do what.

Again, I followed these conversations with additional correspondence detailing my response to their arguments: I explained that in determining the fine I considered several factors: the impact the violation had on the surrounding environment (i.e. the size of the area affected and how long the violation existed), if as a general contractor, he was in a position to know the applicable laws, was there a financial gain as a result of the activities, record of previous violations, and their cooperation in resolving the violation (which included the expenses incurred for reclamation). In addition, the legislature established a range of fines for violations of environmental laws from $100 to $10,000 per day for each day a violation exists. (I did not consider the penalty to be overly burdensome as it was only twelve times the cost of the normal application fee.)

However, I expressed a willingness to negotiate the amount of the penalty. I also enclosed copies of correspondence from my colleagues concerning the other nearby sites brought to our attention earlier.

A couple of weeks after that letter was sent, I personally got a call from the contractor's state representative. He said the contractor felt frustrated because the landowners were not cooperating with him or each other. I told him I can understand his frustration, but my goal is just to get the site into compliance with the laws of the State, either through a permit or implementation of a closing plan. He basically gave me an earful of how he felt I was not respectful to the defendants. I apologized for conveying that perception but it was not my intention and I promised to call the contractor.

When I spoke with the contractor, he went into his litany of how he was being persecuted while everyone else in the countryside was getting away with something. He even felt that I was not treating him "right," would not speak with him, and was picking on him. I said I was sorry he felt that way, but I had other violations of a similar type I was pursuing far more vigorously than this one; just because they were not near you does not mean we are not addressing other violations. I also emphasized that the law had been broken and I was trying to bring the site into compliance. He closed without committing to do anything but went on to say he thought that his representative would be arranging a meeting for him with the Commissioner. He promised to call me back.

In the fall, almost one year after being assigned the case, an unexpected development arose: I received a call from a consultant who was putting together an application for a new borrow pit on a piece of property bordering the parcel that was under investigation. This new partnership was considering incorporating the land of one of the defendants (who owned a third of the violative site) into their project. They wanted to know what I thought about this proposal. If the permit was approved this would bring that part of the site into compliance. I thought this would be a great (partial) solution. While this new partnership would bear the cost of remediation of the older operation, I think they benefited because they could use the existing access road. However, he did not know what the other property owner was going to do, he had not reached an agreement with him.

Two weeks later the state representative called me again. His constituent was still upset because neither of the landowners was cooperating with him (the contractor). I thought it would be to their advantage to work together. Although it was not my call to decide who would take what share of the responsibility, it would make my job easier, so I told him I would see what I could do. I contacted both of the landowners who assured me that the contractor had an engineer working on a plan and the site would be reclaimed in the spring.

The next time I spoke with the contractor, several months later, I was perplexed when he told me that he was still upset about the fine and he did not want to pay for the reclamation of the site. He thought the Department staff would organize a meeting with the adjacent partnership and the town to take over the site. This was news to me. It was obvious I was being lied to by someone. So, with approximately eighteen months invested in this case, I wrote another letter, as much to make a record of its current status, as to communicate with the parties.

In this one, I reiterated that the purpose of the enforcement action was to bring the site into compliance. Their options were to close and reclaim the area; or obtain a permit on their own or in partnership with the new operation. I requested a written response in two weeks as to what course of action they intended to pursue in order to revise the consent agreement. I went on to say that if

I did not receive a response, I would have to consider raising the monetary penalty and/or referring the case to the Office of the Attorney General for resolution.

In response, the contractor called me to arrange a meeting to resolve the situation. He had not heard from the landowners but wanted to meet anyway. I agreed to meet and suggested he bring his engineer/consultant, attorney if he had one, and the landowners. He said he would be back in touch with me. The meeting did not happen any time soon. The contractor became very ill and the landowners never responded. I became distracted by other cases and could not focus on this case until the summer. After making a recovery, the contractor called me and told me he thought the adjacent property owner amended their permit to include their operation. Upon review of Department records, and discussions with the project analyst, I determined that approximately six acres of the violative site were licensed under this new permit and therefore in compliance. However, that left approximately twelve acres not addressed. The contractor then requested an opportunity to investigate the status of the operation and would get back in touch with me.

It was already October, almost two years into the case, so I wrote what I thought was a reasonable letter stating that resolution had been delayed, by all parties involved, far too long and the purpose of this correspondence was to provide notice that we should be able to reach an agreement by the end of the calendar year or I would have no choice but to refer the matter to the Attorney General.

I received no immediate response, but with the end of the year fast approaching, the contractor called me to arrange a meeting. We set a time for him to come to the office in mid-December. At the appointed time he arrived with his wife, current and former members of the town planning board, and his state representative.

I thought the meeting was just going to be between me and him. If I knew he was bringing a crowd, I would have had some colleagues join me as well. The representative began by explaining he just wanted his constituent to get a fair hearing, he was not trying to evade his responsibility or liability, but he was not getting any cooperation from the other parties. The contractor was more blunt; he said he was being jerked around by the property owners. They would not allow him access to the property to reclaim it, or to make plans to do so, nor would they even discuss potential solutions with him. I pretty much listened and said that I can only base a decision on the information I have available and knowing that none of you are working together toward a solution would have a big impact on how I would pursue compliance. This was the first time he had come out and told me the landowners were totally uncooperative. All along everyone indicated they were making progress. After their opportunity to vent, I told them I would take this new information into consideration and consult with my superiors on a course of action.

At this point, since it was everyman for himself, we decided to draft three separate consent agreements. As the contractor did not own the land, nor have immediate access to it, we assessed him a penalty of two thousand dollars, one third of what we were originally asking. In March, he accepted just to get this behind him and signed the consent agreement. Actually he got a good deal, it would cost a lot more than this to reclaim the site but since he was not a landowner we could not make him do that.

The landowners were another story; neither of them wanted to pay a penalty. In the spring of the new year, I received a call from an attorney who was a partner in the new neighboring operation. He wanted to negotiate on the defendant landowners behalf; stating that he did not feel it was appropriate for them to pay a penalty. He even forwarded a letter to me further detailing his arguments.

I responded that a permit had only been issued for a portion of the violative site and the punitive portion of the case had not been resolved. I indicated I was left with no alternative but to request that the Board refer the case to the Office of the Attorney General at their regular meeting in June.

Prior to the meeting the attorney from the partnership called again, this time maintaining that we were letting the contractor off in response to political pressure and intervention from the legislature. I maintained that this was not what happened; I tried unsuccessfully for over two years to reach a consensus with all three parties and after that time I realized no such thing was going to occur. Everyone was pretty much stringing me along. That is why we decided to pursue three separate actions: no one could blame someone else for delays or say the other person was handling it. He also asked me to apply pressure to the contractor to agree to reclaim the site.

The consent agreement for the contractor and the referral of the two landowners to the Attorney General was put on the Board's agenda and scheduled to go before them in June. They decided to not vote on any of the items to allow us one more chance to negotiate settlements.

With the imminent referral of their case to the Attorney General, the landowner with the permit agreed to sign the consent agreement and pay a two thousand dollar penalty.

I also received a call from an attorney representing the second landowner. I indicated I thought he already had counsel. It turned out the other attorney was not representing the landowners but was representing his own interests as a partner of the new neighboring operation. Here I was thinking he was trying to negotiate a settlement on the violator's behalf. Although his partnership was going to take over part of this violative operation, I believe he figured he could save money by having us force the contractor to reclaim the site.

Since this case was so sensitive, with the oversight of a legislator, and the parties challenging the way it was handled, the Commissioner's staff did a great job of briefing the Board prior to the meeting. The only question that arose was why the case dragged on for so long. The Deputy Commissioner, who was present at the meeting, responded that negotiations in some cases could take several years due to the many issues and parties involved. The partner/lawyer also requested to address the Board. Since he was not representing any of the parties with business before the Board they refused to hear him. The Board voted unanimously to accept the two consent agreements and the referral of the third party.

As I was leaving the meeting, the partner tried to get me to discuss the case with him. I was angry since he deceived me so I told him I could no longer discuss the case as the Attorney General now had the lead for its resolution. Although we never pursued it, as an attorney, misrepresenting his participation as counsel to the defendants in a case was to say the least unethical, if not altogether illegal.

This case was the one I actually had as part of my caseload for the longest period of time: not quite three years. And even then it was not totally resolved. It demonstrates how complicated negotiations can get with multiple defendants, as well as, external political pressures. With a legislator speaking up for them, one of the defendants felt he did not necessarily have to comply with my requests to resolve the violation. In addition, the defendants, along with the legislator felt they were being harshly treated, while on the other hand the partner in the neighboring operation accused me of letting the contractor off the hook. In the face of these arguments the fact that I always emphasized, in all the conversations and correspondence I had with the affected parties, was that a violation of the law existed, you caused it, and my goal was compliance with the law. While at times the case was frustrating, I knew we were right and I had the evidence to prove it. No one ever questioned whether there was a violation, but resorted to process issues, such as my handling of the case, or what someone else was doing to deflect attention away from their responsibility.

CHAPTER 8

SITE DEVELOPMENT

I received a complaint that someone was allegedly developing a residential subdivision on Birch Island in Harpswell that required a State development permit.

This case generated a lot of interest in the Town because it involved the subdivision of island property into small lots that were being sold as sites for summer homes. There was a concern that the developer was possibly exploiting coastal property by proposing a project whose density would generate adverse impacts on the fragile Island environment. Even before I began my investigation a reporter from a local paper, the Brunswick Times Record, inquired what the Department's position on the project was. I informed him I had no comment because I had not had a chance to begin my investigation.

I began the investigation by calling a member of the Harpswell Planning Board to get the history of the site. In August, of the previous year, the alleged violator received local planning board approval for the subdivision of a parcel measuring nineteen and three quarter acres in size on the westerly peninsula of Birch Island into ten lots. The Town's approval process required a property survey, site drawings, and proof of ownership and proper soils to site septic systems. The Board also tries to go out to visit the site. Then a vote is held. If approval is given, as it was here, the Board did not track the property after that. Coincidentally, all of these lots had been offered for sale at around fifty thousand dollars apiece, through the same realtor selling the house in the Stream Crossing case in chapter one. Since the subdivision was less than twenty acres in size it appeared the State may not have jurisdiction.

A couple of weeks later, our office received a call from an Inland Fish and Wildlife Chief Warden who purchased a lot there. He heard rumors that the development may be subject to State regulation and wanted to make sure the law was followed. We made an appointment to meet at the Denny's in South Portland to discuss what he knew. Over coffee he explained it was his impression that the lot he bought was part of the first phase of a larger project that would eventually involve more than the nineteen acres currently for sale. He also thought several family members were partners in the project. He gave me the name of an Assistant Attorney General who he thought may have been involved in a transaction. I called him and he said he attended the closing of the sale on one of the lots. He asked if I knew what the sellers plans were as they owned over a hundred acres comprising one end of the island. It was also his impression that it was a family enterprise and they indicated that they did not feel State permits or approvals would be necessary to sell additional lots.

With these tips as an incentive, I made visits to the town office and the Cumberland County Registry of Deeds to research the public record of the Island property. I was able to determine that during the previous summer, three siblings purchased approximately sixty acres (from which the ten lots totaling 19.75 acres described earlier were offered for sale) on Birch Island's westerly peninsula and received an exclusive option to purchase seventy four acres on the easterly peninsula.

In November, they sold the option for the seventy four acres to their mother. In December, she exercised it by purchasing the seventy four acres. In February, the mother received local planning board approval for a nine lot nineteen acre subdivision on the easterly peninsula. See Figure 6 for site drawing. The drawing for the subdivision was recorded in the plan book at the County Registry. In June, she received preliminary approval from the local planning board to subdivide the remaining fifty five acres of the easterly peninsula.

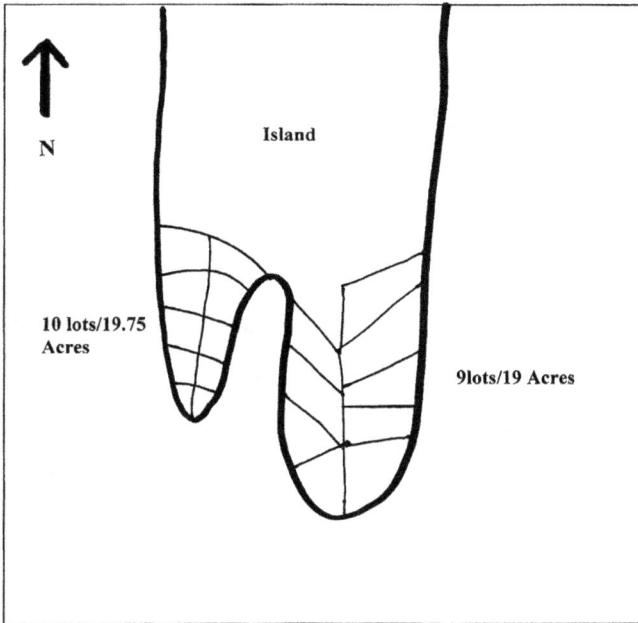

Figure 6 – Birch Island Subdivisions

After reviewing the above facts with the Office of the Attorney General, it was determined that the mother's purchase of the option and property on the easterly peninsula were transactions that took place to circumvent the law. According to the State regulations they were all considered a single "person" and the one hundred thirty four acres they owned was a single "parcel of land." Therefore, the offering for sale of the children's nineteen plus acre subdivision on the westerly peninsula of Birch Island, and the receipt of local planning board approval and the recording of a subdivision plot plan for the mother's nineteen acre subdivision on the easterly peninsula, were overt acts in furtherance of an intent to construct a subdivision of at least thirty eight acres in size. As such, the State acquired jurisdiction over the subdivisions on the east and west peninsulas of Birch Island.

We pursued a consent agreement in this case because we felt the family members involved had made a conscious effort to try to utilize multiple transactions to evade the law. In addition, since the case generated a lot of publicity we felt we could not back off but had to bring the site into compliance.

In August, I summarized these facts and drafted a letter to the attorneys the landowners had retained. We proposed resolving the violation by having them file a permit application. The application should include the two nineteen acre subdivisions, as well as, any other acreage within the one hundred thirty four acre parcel which they intend to subdivide or otherwise develop. We also stated that no additional lots should be sold until a permit is obtained.

We were prepared to discuss allowing the completion of sales of the lots in the first nineteen acre subdivision on the westerly peninsula provided they agree in the context of a consent agreement, that the law applies to the entire parcel and to take the following actions:

1. Immediately file an application for the one hundred thirty four acres,
2. Adhere to the terms and conditions of any permit,
3. Notify all purchasers of the lots in the first subdivision that State approval for the subdivision has not been obtained, that any approval may require changes be made to the subdivision, and the landowners could be responsible for making these changes,
4. Pay a monetary penalty.

Their initial response was that we were "reaching" to establish jurisdiction over the site. Even though several members of the same family were involved they maintained their business affairs were separate. To maintain their charade that they were not working together, the mother and siblings each hired their own counsel from different law firms.

After spending the better part of the summer investigating the case and trying to negotiate with their attorneys; my supervisor felt we should not spend any more time on it and just refer the case to the Attorney General's Office for disposition as they saw fit. It was obvious they did not want to negotiate with us. Referring a case to the Attorney General's Office did not mean it would automatically go to court, but for recalcitrant parties it did elevate the negotiations to another level. We felt this was necessary because one of the defendant's attorneys specialized in dealing with the Department and we could tell he was stalling.

We decided to appear before the Board to inform them of our plan to refer the case. To put an issue before the Board you forwarded a memo summarizing it which was placed in a package of background materials for their biweekly meetings. The meetings were usually held in the state capitol of Augusta, but were sometimes convened in other parts of the State. I had introduced consent agreements on other occasions but they were pretty much self-explanatory and no questions were asked of me. When items were to be presented to the Board I typically notified the affected parties involved so they could attend if they desired. I asked my supervisor if we should notify the attorneys. Against my better judgment he said not to bother because we did not necessarily need the Board's permission for the referral. He saw it more as a courtesy; that we were informing them of the issues in the case and were merely providing notice that the Attorney General's Office was to be the lead from now on.

In late August, the Board met in a pine paneled hotel basement in the Town of Norway. Even though we did not notify them of the referral, one of the defendant's attorneys was in attendance. As I said earlier, he was very familiar with the Department's operations and probably reviewed a copy of the Board's public agenda; it is usually put together a day or two before the meeting so the members can review the issues for their consideration. When the item came up for discussion we both stepped forward.

He could have removed the item for discussion by saying he was not notified of the item going before them today. For one reason or another he did not do this. He probably did not want to totally embarrass me in order to maintain a working relationship. He argued that discussions with the Department should continue and the referral was not necessary.

The acting Chairman asked the Commissioner's opinion; he said, "I'm not familiar with the case so I can't make a recommendation." The Chairman turned to me and chewed me out for not adequately preparing the Commissioner for such an "important matter." I felt bad for blowing the presentation, but upon reflection of subsequent events put it in the perspective that the Chairman was trying to ingratiate himself to the regulated community. When he eventually resigned from the Board, he became a "consultant" specializing in representing clients with business before the Department.

Many of the Board members were under the mistaken impression that a referral to the Attorney General's Office was tantamount to their making a finding of guilt and a court action would follow. Either the Commissioner or I should have explained that the Attorney General's Office did not have to take the case to court but that their skill in negotiation combined with their ability to proceed to court was needed. I did not speak up aggressively because I was worried about the Board being told that the other party was not given "proper notice" about the day's meeting. A vote on the issue was postponed until the Commissioner could make an informed recommendation to the Board.

A colleague from my office was attending the meeting on another matter and we left together to go to lunch. He could not believe that the Commissioner did not speak up that notwithstanding the facts of the case the referral was a courtesy and was for informational purposes only. I felt pretty low at this point. My supervisor hit the roof when I told him what happened; he was mad at me, but also at the acting Commissioner for not speaking up. Nevertheless, other events forced a resolution to the case regardless of the Board's inaction.

The next day I got a call from a perspective buyer. The defendants were still trying to sell the remaining lots in the first nineteen acre subdivision, but the investigation scared everyone off. Who wants to buy into a development that is illegal and you may get stuck paying for some type of remediation. He said the sellers told him they would do whatever it takes to get the lots freed up. At fifty thousand dollars apiece the developer had an incentive to resolve the situation. Even if he felt they did not need permits, potential buyers were not interested in the property unless they had some assurance as to the safety of their investment.

Even though the Board did not approve the referral, the Attorney General's Office took over the lead in the negotiations anyway. Two weeks after the Board meeting, I found myself in a conference room at Headquarters with our Division Director, the Assistant Attorney General assigned to the case and the defendant's attorneys. The opposing counsel started off with a sarcastic request demanding that we prostrate ourselves for, among other things, not informing them of the meeting at which the referral was discussed and the way in which the case was generally handled. My Division Director responded that while notice should have been given, we would not under any circumstances prostrate ourselves for anyone. In contrast to my experience with the Commissioner, this was more like it: back-up from the top. She recognized we had a good case and wanted to negotiate a settlement. This was particularly evident because the attorney's first line of defense was to attack our process not the facts.

With those pleasantries out of the way they proposed a solution. They maintained their clients' ignorance of State jurisdiction when the development began but still wanted to finish selling the lots from the first nineteen acre subdivision. They offered to rescind the subsequent approvals and pay a penalty. The Division Director and Assistant Attorney General left the room to discuss the offer. I stayed and chatted with the Attorneys. We all knew this was a complex and difficult case due to the numerous parties, parcels of land, local approvals, buyers and potential buyers involved to date. The purchasers wanted answers and the seller wanted cash. It was my turn to be sarcastic; I asked if they had a lot of cases like this. They chuckled and admitted it was an unusual one for them too. My Division Director returned and agreed to accept the terms. The Assistant Attorney General drafted a consent decree stating the violation, their agreement to rescind the local planning board approvals, admit they were subject to the law if they expanded the subdivision beyond the first nineteen acres, and would obtain a permit prior to doing so. The penalty was sixty three hundred dollars.

After all was said and done I felt good about the outcome. Due to my investigation and legwork, a settlement favorable to the Department was negotiated in that we were able to assert jurisdiction over a potentially large development on a small island. We also generated a lot of local publicity on the law and its requirements.

I learned how important it is to keep everyone informed every step of the way while developing a case and maneuvering it through the system. During the Board meeting, I could have been raked over the coals more than I was if the attorney mentioned he had not been directly notified of the agenda item concerning his client. Due to that fear, I was pretty much neutralized and the opposition won a delay. In the end it did not have much effect on the outcome of the case; the Attorney General's Office still took over the lead and negotiated the settlement. If anything, it gave the Department a reason to put the case behind us quickly. This case was settled six months after I received the complaint.

CHAPTER 9

SOLID WASTE

Americans generate more than two hundred fifty million tons of trash per year. Since 1960, the overall trend we have witnessed is a rise in both the total tons of waste generated and pounds generated per person. Government typically regulates the location, operation, design, and closure of solid waste facilities due to adverse environmental and public health impacts that have been linked to poor disposal practices. These impacts usually result from surface water (i.e. streams, rivers, lakes) and groundwater contamination. Groundwater is water that naturally flows through and is stored in soil and rocks. It is a major source of drinking water and of water used for agriculture. Almost half of this country's population depends upon ground water for some or all of its drinking water. Once ground water is contaminated it is very costly to clean up.

Contamination can occur when liquids (usually rainwater) move through waste disposal sites and into the surrounding waters, carrying pollutants with them. The resulting mixture of liquid and pollutant is called leachate. Contaminants in the buried refuse may result from the disposal of industrial wastes, ash, waste treatment sludge, hazardous waste, or from normal household waste decomposition. The composition of leachate varies greatly from site to site, and can vary within a particular site. Some factors affecting its composition include: age of the landfill, type of waste, degree of decomposition. Sometimes it can be seen as reddish orange deposits of bacteria, or oily films on water surfaces.

Runoff from the landfill can contaminate surface waters and groundwater directly, at or near the site. At the end of a facility's useful life, to minimize leachate formation a waste site must be properly closed to limit any potential adverse affects. Closure involves capping a site with a low-permeability material (usually clay or plastic liner) to minimize moisture infiltration. The top layer of soil must support vegetation which also promotes runoff. Berms and grading are also used to control runoff and contamination.

PRATT'S BROOK

I received an anonymous complaint that someone was dumping tree stumps and other debris near the caller's house. The waste was being dumped down an embankment on a vacant lot directly across the street. They had been doing it quite a while and the truck traffic was getting to be a nuisance. The site was on North Road in North Yarmouth.

On a rainy July day I drove out to find the site. I went along North Road until I came to the dump site which was visible as I drove by. I parked on a side road almost directly across from it. The caller must have lived along this street. I stuffed my tape measure and camera into my coat pockets and walked across the road. It was really too warm for a coat but I kept it on because of the rain and to carry my equipment.

Crossing the street, I noticed there was a cable across the entrance to the lot to control access to it. I could see fresh tire tracks in the soft earth which led directly to a couple of piles of stumps, rocks, and soil in an open area that looked to be about a quarter acre lot surrounded by trees and fields. From the road it did not look like very much waste. I walked past these small piles to the back of the lot, away from the road, where I could see the edge of an embankment. When I got there I realized that I was standing on the edge of a cliff of stumps, branches and other wood. It was a forty foot drop. The dirt lot was actually the top of a big pile of wood waste that was covered with a veneer of soil.

From my vantage point, at the top of the pile, I also noticed a stream not far from its base. It looked as if the waste was placed between the road and the brook. The undergrowth around the pile was very thick so I decided to climb down the face of the wood pile to measure how high it was. Then, by measuring the length and width at the top I could estimate the volume of material that had been dumped. I also had to go down to see how far the waste was from the stream.

When I got to the bottom I could see there was a rocky brook about twenty feet wide and a foot or so deep. After taking some pictures that showed the exposed face of debris, I clipped the end of my steel tape to a branch in the base of the pile and made my way through the brush toward the brook. At a hundred feet I was almost to the brook. I yanked the end of the tape free and wound it up. I hooked it on another branch and went another twenty feet to the edge of the brook. It was only one hundred twenty feet from the base of the waste to the edge of the brook.

State law did not allow this type of waste to be dumped within three hundred feet of a body of water. It was barely three hundred feet from the edge of the road to the stream bank. The entire pile of waste was within the buffer area. From down below, it looked easier to go through the woods to get back up to the top of the pile. I walked around to the left and from this perspective, you could tell that there was a giant wedge of wood waste that had been piled onto a steep embankment that dropped off from the road's edge. See Figure 7.

I was wet and muddy after having spent an hour measuring, climbing and photographing the site to document its content and location. When I got to the dirt area on top I was surprised to see a large green truck dumping a load of dirt, rocks and stumps

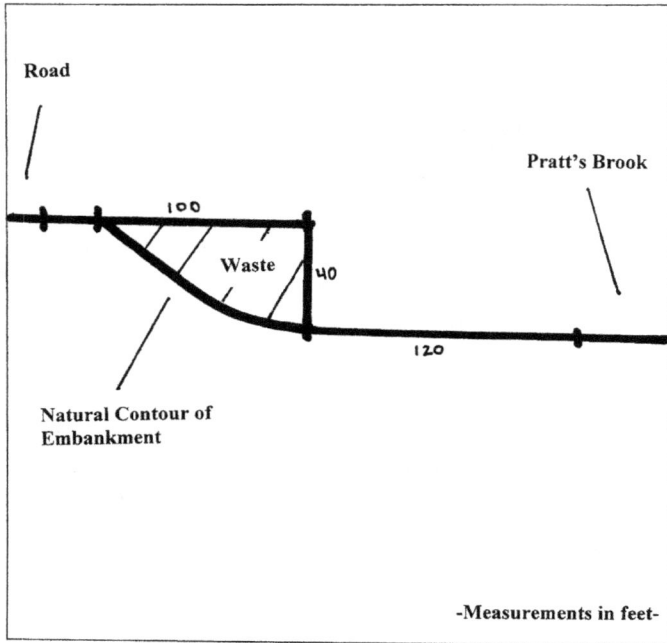

Figure 7 – Cross Section of North Road Site

onto the clearing next to the small piles I noticed when I first arrived. The driver was just as surprised to see me come up from the woods below.

I introduced myself, and explained that I was investigating the property as the result of an anonymous complaint. I informed him that it was a violation of State law to dump this type of material within three hundred feet of a brook. He explained that he did not own the property. A friend of his did and they did not know it was prohibited. He was a contractor who built roads and sewers. He was disposing of materials from land clearing activities. They were using the waste to level the property off because it was so steep. I got his name and address, as well as the property owners, and told him not to dump anything else there. I also explained I would be consulting with my superiors about the possibility of taking some type of enforcement action. He did not say much; I think he felt bad because he got his friend in trouble.

I decided to go back to the office because I was soaked through and covered with mud. At the time, I had only been on the job a couple of months and I felt good about the thoroughness of my investigation and how confidently I handled the violator. It helped that I caught him "red-handed" and I could tell he felt guilty.

Back at the office, I went over the findings of my investigation with my supervisor. We agreed that this would be a good case for formal enforcement action. We had a well documented violation where we actually caught the violator in the act. A lot of the times with these dumping cases you find piles of stuff in the middle of nowhere and cannot figure out where it came from.

The following week I forwarded a letter to the contractor outlining the violation, repeating my request that he not dump on the site anymore, and informing him the State would be taking enforcement action. In August, I forwarded another letter outlining the proposed provisions of the agreement which called for removal of all waste, disposal at an approved site, revegetation of the site on North Road, and payment of a penalty.

Seeking removal of all the debris and revegetating the site were not insignificant conditions. Based upon my measurements, I calculated there were approximately nine thousand cubic yards of waste there. This is equivalent to five hundred large dump truck loads of material. During our discussions I discovered the waste resulted from eighteen months worth of work by his company. While he owned some of the necessary equipment to do the job it would also be a significant investment of time and money. He would likely have to pay a disposal fee at another facility as well.

After asking for the removal of all the waste, he asked what other options he had available. In September, we met on the site again with the property owner. He was an older fellow who was quiet and let the contractor do most of the talking. It seemed since he got them in this mess he was responsible for getting them out. I explained that he could try to get a permit for the site but it was unlikely it would be approved due to the proximity of the stream which was known as Pratt's Brook.

Site restrictions involving solid waste facilities are specific and comprehensive in nature. For example, the solid waste boundary is well within the three hundred foot minimum setback from a body of water. Any deposited waste must also be at least five feet above the seasonal high water table. Due to the proximity of the stream this was not likely the case at this site. Consequently, site restrictions may be too severe to permit approval of a permit.

He did hire an engineer who, in late November, put forth a proposal to remove about a third of the waste, covering the remainder with topsoil, and planting grass on it. Their argument was that the site was too steep to remove all the material without building a road next to the stream. I agreed with them that it would be preferable not to destroy the remaining natural vegetative buffer and there was the potential to create a big mess. I forwarded the plan to our engineering staff at Headquarters so they could review and comment on the proposal. They asked for some changes. The plan was finalized in July of the following year. The plan called for removal of thirty five hundred cubic yards of the waste and disposal of it at the town landfill.

As for the penalty, he admitted to using the dump for a period of eighteen months. If a judge ever found in our favor at one hundred dollars a day, that would be forty five thousand dollars. I will be the first to admit this is out of line for the circumstances surrounding the case, but again, it gives all parties a perspective to negotiate from. Due to his cooperation, and in light of the cleanup expenses, we assessed a penalty of two thousand dollars.

By the time we negotiated the remediation plan, penalty, and the agreement was approved by all parties, fourteen months had passed from when I first discovered the violation. We gave them until the following July, almost two years to the day after we first met to restore the site. I did do a follow up inspection, the site was closed, graded, and revegetated. The slope looked a lot more natural and I was surprised to see how much material had been removed.

This case illustrated to the complainant that the government could be responsive to their concerns. I never found out who they were but I gave them my name when I had spoken to them. They called me back when the equipment showed up to remove the waste. They mistakenly thought the site was being used for disposal again and were pleased when I told them I had arranged for steps to be taken for the site to be cleaned up and properly closed.

CHICKEN FARM

During the summer field season, a typical day could easily involve conducting inspections of six or eight complaints. This could mean that you were on the road driving around all day long. The stops could be short and sweet: no violation or activity the State had jurisdiction over. There could also be contentious conflicts with angry landowners and contractors. It got to be stressful not knowing what to expect. A welcome management tool was being able to set your own schedule. If you were tired of being out for several days in a row you could stay in the office. There was always plenty of work to do there.

One mid-summer day I planned to stay in the office. Everyone else was either going on the road or preparing for meetings so I was going to do my paperwork and cover the phones.

It was not even 8:30a.m., when our supervisor received a call from Headquarters that there was an emergency in the small rural town of Dayton. Someone from our office had to go down there to represent the Department. Two large barns at an egg farm burned down to the ground. The barns contained a hundred thousand chickens. There were no survivors. All the chickens were half burnt like bad barbecue; black on the outside and raw on the inside. The Department had to help locate a suitable disposal site before they became a health hazard. In the middle of summer the warm weather would putrefy the carcasses. Since everyone else had scheduled appointments I had to go.

It was a good forty five minute drive to the farm. I could smell the burnt chicken about a mile from the place. Besides the smell, I was met there by the owner, a representative from the State Department of Agriculture (DOA), and a scientist from the Soil Conservation Service (SCS). The DOA was involved because of the issue of farm animal disposal, the SCS would help locate a geologically suitable site, and my job was to make sure the site met state guidelines. For example, we did not want the waste dumped where it could contaminate someone's well water. I had never met any of these individuals before, but the three of us working together were supposed to develop options for the disposal of all the chickens and what was left of the buildings as soon as possible.

After spending a few minutes looking over the remains of the chickens and the barns we had to figure out what to do next. The scientist suggested we go to the local SCS field office to locate a soil survey of the immediate area which would give us a general idea of the local geology. We were trying to locate impermeable soils, typically containing clay, that would minimize the flow of any contamination from the waste into the groundwater.

The egg farmer owned about half the land in town which included several hundred acres where the barns were located. A review of the soil maps showed that all the land the farmer owned was situated on sand and gravel aquifers: the exact opposite of the type of site we needed. His land was a very poor disposal site because it was a groundwater recharge area and a good source of drinking water. Any chicken juice would percolate straight to the groundwater supply. Since this was a rural area most people in the area were on well water.

That left us with the option of the town dump. It was established before the passage of the State waste management laws and was located on the edge of the aquifer. It was not the optimum spot, but in an emergency it would do. We calculated that one existing source of contamination would be better that creating a new one.

We went out to take a look at the dump. It was down a dirt road not very far from the farm. The dump was basically a mound covering approximately one and a half acres that stood about ten feet tall. Most of the waste was covered with soil except for a pile of tires and another of old appliances. The Department saw this as an acceptable alternative so long as the solid waste boundary was not expanded and the waste was properly covered. The boundary could not be expanded because at the time there was a Statewide moratorium on the permitting of new solid waste facilities or expanding existing ones while the laws were undergoing revision. We told the egg farmer the dump was acceptable to us. However, there was still one small problem: the town had to agree to accept the waste.

By law, the town was required to provide for the disposal of "normal" (i.e. household) waste generated by its residents. A hundred thousand chickens was definitely a special waste that the town did not have to accept if they did not want to. The farmer contacted the Town Selectmen[8] to put in his request. Due to the potential health hazard, and the numerous complaints concerning odors, they agreed to hold an emergency meeting on whether to accept the waste. No one asked me to attend the meeting, so I went back to the office to let my supervisor know what happened.

The next morning, I got another call from Headquarters. They wanted to know why I did not show up at the Selectmen's meeting. I explained that they did not indicate they needed my participation. It turned out the Selectmen wanted to hear the options from us, not the farmer. I guess they did not trust him. They rescheduled the meeting for that night. I was told to attend to represent the Department.

I thought I better get prepared and think about what to say. I found the file on the town dump to familiarize myself with the information we had available. The file consisted of old inspection reports that did not tell me a whole lot I did not already know from looking around there myself. There was no evidence of groundwater contamination but little testing had previously been conducted. Later that afternoon, I met up with my two colleagues from DOA and SCS to review what we would say at the meeting. The farmer expected us to lobby for him to be able to use the dump. Over dinner at the local diner, we agreed our presentation would be to brief the Selectmen on the options available, but the decision was to be theirs. We would tell them there was not an appropriate site on the farmer's property due to the nature of the soils in the area and that the dump was a suitable site. In the alternative, the waste could be transported (at great expense to the farmer) to a commercial facility. Since time was a factor, this was problematic if the farmer was short on cash and it could take time to negotiate a contract.

We arrived together at the Town Hall and found the meeting room. Two local television stations sent news crews with cameras to cover the meeting. There were five selectmen. We introduced ourselves and I sat down at one end of the table with them. The DOA guy sat in the audience of about thirty townspeople and the scientist sat off to the side near me. At the time, I did not realize that this was to be a public hearing where people could comment, otherwise I would not have sat at the table. I thought we were going to meet and discuss the issue with the selectmen and the public could observe. Was I wrong.

The Head Selectman called the meeting to order and explained the issue to be decided. They first asked what we thought. The DOA representative began with a statement that time was of the essence to dispose of the birds in a sanitary manner. Although they had been burned, it was far from complete, there was still a lot of flesh inside the birds that would become putrid in the summer heat. Next, the soil scientist gave a brief presentation on his opinion why there was not a suitable site in the area. I explained the Department's position "The dump is a suitable site so long as the waste boundary is not expanded." I also went over what should be done if the waste was accepted: it would have to be placed on the existing mound, compacted (run over with a bulldozer), covered with two feet of clay, then soil and seeded with grass. It would also be a good idea to install a couple of monitoring wells to track any groundwater contamination.

One of the Selectmens' concerns was that if they accepted the waste the State would then order the immediate closure of the dump because it was filled to capacity. They wanted an assurance that the Department would not close it as a result of taking the farmer's waste. I explained that I was not authorized to make such a guarantee on the spot but I could check on it and get back to them. He sarcastically asked " Why did they send someone who can't make a decision." In hindsight, I think he was a little miffed that I was at the table with them, no one told me not to sit there, so I stayed.

Before they were to vote they opened the meeting up to public comment. The first guy to speak said the farmer was a crook and should not be allowed to use the dump. It was obvious he hated the farmer. Although I didn't have to, I responded we were just trying to find an appropriate site to dispose of the waste and the dump was the closest one. A few other people spoke; they didn't care where it went so long as it was taken care of quickly. They lived nearby and could smell it.

At the end of the comments they voted to accept the waste with three conditions: 1. the Town needed to receive a written assurance from the Department that the dump would not be closed as a result of accepting the waste; 2. the farmer hire an engineer to supervise the waste disposal so it did not undermine the integrity of the dump; and 3. he also had to put in two test wells and monitor them. Everyone thought that was reasonable. As my supervisor later said "The town could make the farmer paint his house blue if they wanted to."

The next day I called Headquarters to fill them in about the meeting including the town's request for a letter. They said fine. The letter, which my supervisor signed, stated that the Town could continue to accept waste until such time as the dump is evaluated for closure and remediation by the Department which was previously scheduled to occur by the end of the following year. I called the Town's attorney and read him the letter. He said remove the date by when the Department would conduct its review and they would accept it. I revised the letter and drove it down to the attorney's office to deliver it. He accepted it.

Later that afternoon I received a call from the farmer's engineer. We made an appointment to meet the next day to review their disposal plan. After moving the tires and appliances off to the side he proposed to build a three sided berm three feet high which would cover half the dump. They would fill that with the waste, compact it, and cover it. If needed, they would build a similar berm on the other half as well. They began work on Monday, a week after the fire, and had all the chickens in the ground by Friday. I went out to inspect the dump three weeks later and it was all covered and graded; no smell. The waste took up less room than we thought. The engineer said it all compacted real well. You could not tell there were one hundred thousand chickens there.

I knew I was doing a good job, when after three days of working with the DOA representative he said he liked working with me. He thought I was realistic and willing to be innovative by adapting to the situation. Our solution may not have been the best option, but it was practical and was better for the community than the status quo of letting the chickens fester. It could have easily developed into a health problem and it was already a nuisance.

CHAPTER 10

PERMIT VIOLATIONS

All of the violations presented so far have had several things in common: they involved regulated activities under the jurisdiction of a single law and none of them had been issued permits prior to intervention by enforcement staff. In contrast, the cases presented in this chapter all involve activities that resulted in violations of more than one law and all of the projects had been issued State environmental permits. These cases emphasize the point that obtaining a permit does little to protect the environment if it is not followed. It is necessary for the government to have a presence out in the field to show the regulated community that compliance is required and expected.

SACO RIVER

One of the very first complaints I was assigned to was of an illegal discharge into the Saco River. The source was reportedly the construction site of a solid waste incinerator in an industrial area in the center of Biddeford. The complaint stated that the project involved activity on the shoreline that was causing siltation and fouling the entire River. The complaint was anonymous so I could not get any more details.

The Biddeford-Saco area is the site of former mills that grew from hydro-power generated by a series of dams on the River. At the time, the towns were attempting to revitalize their business centers. One project involved the conversion of an abandoned tannery and shoe factory into condominiums. This former industrial complex, known as Factory Island, was located on the River with several adjacent facilities still in operation.

I went out on a June day to conduct an inspection. Prior to leaving, I did some cursory background research on the area but I was not sure what I was really looking for, or exactly where. I did know that a Fortune 500 Company was under contract to construct a cogeneration plant that would incinerate trash. The heat from the furnace would be used to create steam to generate electricity. It was being constructed on this site because it was an industrial zone and the river would provide a source of water. The project had three State environmental permits (two stream alteration and one site development).

I located the facility and asked a workman who was in charge. I was directed to a foreman. I introduced myself and explained that I wished to inspect the construction activity near the River. He asked if I had any identification. I gave him a freshly minted business card. He looked it over for a minute, then called over to a young guy who he instructed to take me to the River.

One of their permits authorized construction activity on the river bank including the erection of a coffer dam that would enable them to install intake pumps and outflows for the cooling water. A coffer dam is a temporary watertight enclosure that is built along the section of shoreline you need to work on. It allows you to pump the water out from an area to expose the bottom of the body of water so that construction may be undertaken. After you finish, you remove the dam and the work area is flooded once again. See Figure 8.

Their dam was constructed of stone and fill. To keep the area dry behind it required the periodic pumping of water that seeped in. Prior to discharging the water into the River they sent it through a

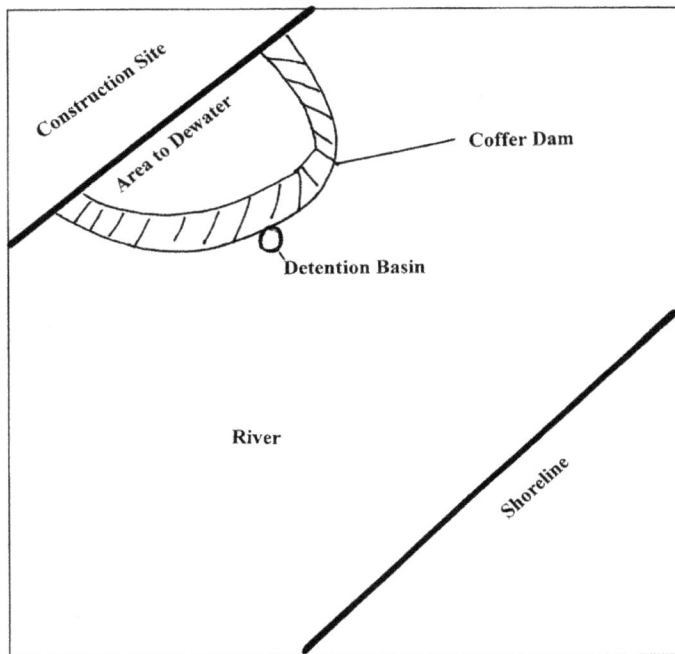

Figure 8 – Coffer Dam Area

small detention basin they built in order to allow any sediment to settle out. During my inspection they were sending it through the basin and a small amount of turbidity was evident in the River but dissipated quickly. The River was at least a hundred feet across and its entire width was not fouled as described in the complaint. I was not sure if it was a violation or not, but it did not look like too big a deal. I thanked them for showing me around and left.

After getting back to the office, I consulted with my supervisor. I described what I saw. We reviewed the permits and it seemed they were complying with them. I did not have a good feel if this was a violation or not so my supervisor suggested we go out together to take a look. He called the company representatives and arranged for us to meet them to go out to take another look. The following day we met their attorney and one of the site engineers. Everything appeared as it did the day before and my supervisor said that was an expected amount of turbidity that had minimal impact on the river. Their activities were in compliance with the permits.

The following week, another caller left a message stating there were major discharges into the River originating from construction in the downtown area. This time I went out to a bridge reconstruction project a quarter mile upstream of the incinerator project. I met with the site foreman who was very cooperative. There was not much activity on the site that day so there were no discharges into the River.

Another week passed. Another call came in regarding discharges into the Saco River. I was in the office that day so it was my first opportunity to speak directly with the caller. I explained that I had been out there three times in the last two weeks, stopped at several spots along the River, and found nothing. He maintained that it was coming from the incinerator site and that they were discharging directly into the River again. I explained that some turbidity was normal with a project such as this; so long as they utilized the sedimentation basin they were in compliance with the law. He responded that he had seen pipes discharging mud directly into the River. I talked him into leaving his name and number and said I would be in touch.

My supervisor did not want me to go out to the incinerator site again because it was a politically sensitive project. It was to be the future solid waste disposal option for many of the communities in the southern portion of the State and he did not want it to seem like we were harassing them. I contacted the caller and told him I would meet him in Biddeford so he could show me what he was talking about. I explained that we would have to be able to view the activity without going onto the incinerator project's property. He said we did not have to.

We made an appointment to meet on Factory Island the next day. He was thirty minutes late and I was about to leave when he showed up. I followed him down a narrow alley that led to the River. We were on the shore opposite the incinerator and sure enough there were five pipes extended over the coffer dam. Of those, two were discharging heavily silted water directly into the River. They were not using the detention basin; the siltation turned the entire River brown.

I explained that this was nothing like what I had seen on my previous visits. This definitely appeared to be a violation of their permits. It turned out the caller was a student at the University of New England who tended a salmon ladder below a downstream dam as part of a school project. He was on the River every day and said it had been like this, on and off, for a month now. He was worried that all the silt was lowering the water quality and keeping salmon from approaching the ladder. I thanked him for showing me the site and said I would be in touch.

Back at the office, I went over what I had seen with my supervisor. He agreed it appeared they violated their permits. He suggested we gather as much documentation together as we could on their recent activities to illustrate the violation. I contacted the student; explaining that we were considering enforcement action and needed his help to build a case. He wanted his name kept out of it. I told him our case would be much stronger with his cooperation; I did not think it necessary to reveal his identity but if I had to I would at least warn him first. He agreed to help. He said he kept a daily field log for his project that included notes on the water conditions. He also took some pictures of pipes from the construction site discharging in the River that he would send to me.

After reviewing the information he forwarded, we estimated that at a minimum, similar discharges occurred during a two week period during the latter part of June. I called the project's attorney confronting her with the alleged violation. She responded that she would have to investigate the activities with the contractor.

She contacted me a few days later to admit that due to unforeseen complications during construction, the contractor was forced to bypass the settlement basin on six different days over a two week period. It's worth highlighting that while they appeared cooperative during my initial inquiries, they did not volunteer this information until I produced evidence based on an eyewitness account.

These discharges were violations of State environmental laws because they ignored the prohibition to discharge any pollutant (including sand, dirt, rock) into waters of the State. As part of our assessment we also scrutinized the permits. A standard condition of approval of the site development permit is that the applicant comply with all applicable permits and federal, state and local laws during the project's construction, which they did not.

The State also issued a stream alteration permit authorizing the construction of the coffer dam. The permit stipulated that when the work areas were to be pumped dry; a settling pond was to be utilized before water re-entered the River. A condition of the permit stated "...sedimentation control measures will be appropriately applied and maintained for effectiveness while work is in progress." A subsequent amendment stated "Anadromous fish runs occur in the Saco River Corridor during June and early July...Siltation of the River during these periods would affect the runs of anadromous fish by altering the quality of the waters of the Saco River. The proposed activity will not unreasonably harm wildlife habitat provided no work is done in the waters of the Saco River between June I and July I..." We felt obligated to assess penalties through a consent agreement because they violated every permit they held.

During the late Summer/early Fall, I drafted the consent agreement. We named the owner of the project as well as their contractor who was constructing the facility as co-defendants. In the fall, I forwarded the agreement which assessed a penalty of sixty thousand dollars (six days of violations at ten thousand dollars per day). We thought it appropriate to seek such a penalty seeing how their permits specifically instructed them against doing what they did.

The project's attorney responded that they would need time to negotiate with the contractor. On a project of this type, the client usually stipulates that it is the contractor's responsibility to conduct all activities in accordance with applicable laws. Due to this "private" agreement, the contractor would end up paying for the penalty out of their pocket. Not surprisingly, the contractor indicated they wanted to contest the agreement.

It was not until the following Spring that we were able to arrange a meeting with the two parties to discuss the penalty. In addition to the corporate representatives, about six attorneys representing the project's principals, the prime contractor, and a subcontractor also attended the meeting. The subcontractor was not named in the agreement but the prime contractor was going to turn around and stick them with the penalty. A Deputy Attorney General and I represented the State.

We let them do most of the talking: Obviously they thought the penalty was too high, especially since the discharges were "unintentional." They promised to forward more detailed information on what actually occurred. We agreed to review this information and take it into consideration.

In May, they forwarded the report. The information was compiled by a review of field logs and interviews with subcontractors involved in the construction of the coffer dam. The report stated that technical difficulties such as power outages and equipment failure resulted in water from behind the coffer dam being pumped directly into the River on five different occasions totaling fifteen to twenty hours. Based upon this information, in consultation with the Attorney General's Office, we lowered the penalty to fifteen thousand dollars.

Since we agreed to lower the penalty and the Deputy Attorney General realized the case was not as big as he thought he lowered it on his list of priorities. It was not until mid-Fall before I could get him to review the revised agreement. Then the defendants requested minor language changes that took several more months for him to approve. It took almost two years to get complete signoff by all the parties.

Although the violation appeared to be blatant, the Deputy Attorney General did not feel we had a strong case to seek a higher penalty because the permit language could be interpreted as allowing some siltation. The use of the sediment basin was acknowledgement that some would occur but that it should be controlled. In addition, at the time there were other projects on the River that may have contributed to some of the turbidity. Finally, we did not have any water samples. While eyewitness accounts were helpful they would not be enough to quantify the impacts to have a judge assess a steep penalty. We preferred to negotiate a lower penalty than take a chance in court.

NONESUCH RIVER

One October, I received a complaint concerning the placement of fill in the Nonesuch River. The property was located near a warehouse of the Humpty Dumpty Potato Chip Company. The directions specified the site was on the Scarborough town line on Route One. I drove out there early in the morning. It was to be my first stop of the day. I intended to visit a half dozen sites in the area. I located the building with little difficulty and parked on the shoulder of the road nearby. I did not expect to find much because I did not immediately see any evidence of construction equipment. I decided to take a quick look around before moving on to my next stop.

I walked along the edge of the parking lot that was nearest the River. It was evident that the building's site had been part of the River's floodplain but it was filled a long time ago to raise the elevation to that of the road. I walked a couple of hundred feet along the embankment and did not spot any construction activity. At the back corner of the lot, I decided to go down onto the floodplain and circle back toward the road by walking along the shoreline to see if there was any activity closer to the River.

The floodplain was covered with shrubs and tall grasses. Irregular paths wound their way through the growth. None of them seemed to go in a direct line to the River which was only a couple hundred feet away. I bushwhacked through the undergrowth and reached the shoreline several minutes later. I took a quick look and noted the River was approximately seventy five feet wide. I found a path that ran along the shoreline and followed it. Although I was only a few feet from the River, I could hardly see the water due to the thick undergrowth. The entire way back I saw no evidence of any activity along the River and figured the complaint was a false alarm.

The path I chose did not go directly back to where my car was parked but, went instead, to the bridge that crossed the River. I climbed up the embankment to the pavement and decided to walk out onto the bridge to take one more look at the area. From this vantage point, I was about thirty feet above the floodplain and would have a good view of both banks of the River. In the middle of the bridge, from this elevated perspective, I was shocked at the color of the water; it was brown with silt. It reminded me of the Saco River the day I saw all the direct discharges going into the water. It was obvious that someone somewhere was discharging something into the River.

Now what to do? It was apparent there was a major problem somewhere upstream. I just inspected the immediate vicinity and did not find evidence of any problems associated with the original complaint.

I always carried a road atlas when I went into the field. I looked at it to scope out the surrounding area. There were several road crossings upstream of my present location. I decided to drive to the next one, on the Gorham Road, to see if the water was the same color as here. If the water was clear, I would know that the source of the siltation was in between these two bridges.

It took twenty minutes to locate the crossing. The River was much narrower there; about thirty feet across. It actually flowed through large corrugated aluminum pipes. It still had the same chocolate color. Since I was a mile upstream of where I first noticed the unusual color of the water I was beginning to think I might have been mistaken; maybe the water is always this color. It did not look quite as bad here because there were a lot of large trees surrounding the crossing so direct sunlight did not hit the water. I took the map out again and located the next crossing. It was about a half mile further upstream, on the Payne Road.

There were not as many large trees around this crossing as the last one. The sun shone brightly. There was no mistaking the turbidity in the water. From the pavement, I noticed that the River forked a short distance upstream. I could not tell if I was at the confluence of two separate channels or if it was just an island. I decided to walk along the shoreline of the left channel first. After going only fifty feet the water was running clear. It only had a slight brown hue that appeared to be from tannin. I realized I might be getting close to something.

I doubled back to the road, crossed the River, and plunged into the undergrowth. I headed for the right channel. Breaking through to the shoreline, I immediately found what I was looking for. From this side, at the confluence of the two branches, you could see the silted water flowing from one branch into the clear water of the other. See Figure 9.

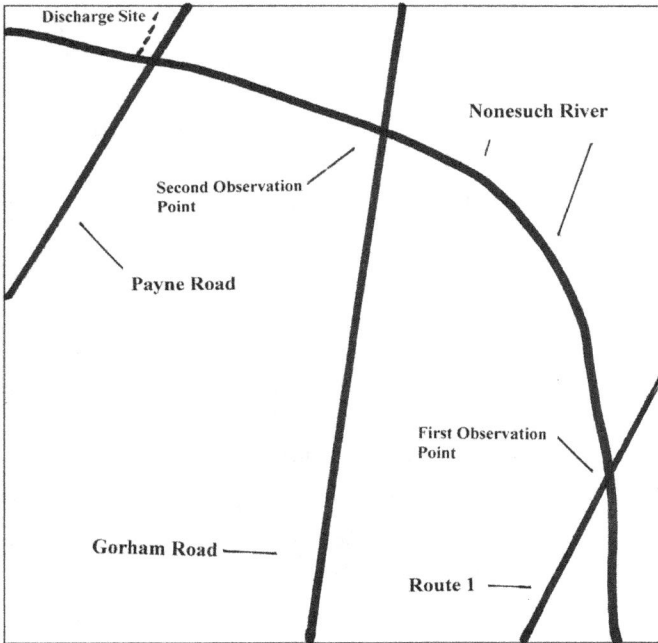

Figure 9 – Nonesuch River Crossing Sites

My pace quickening, I followed the channel upstream. It turned out to be an inlet that ran parallel to the road. It went for a short distance before ending at a narrow floodplain wetland. The wetland bordered a steep embankment. Cutting down the embankment was a small cement gray colored stream. When this mixed with the River water it looked like a light cup of coffee.

I ran back to the car and grabbed my camera. I took a picture where the waters mixed together in the main channel. The difference in color was like night and day; the contrast was unmistakable. I followed the gray stream a couple of hundred yards through the woods. It was surrounded by a mature forest with the undergrowth thinning quickly as I moved away from the River.

I found a blue hose sputtering the gray water directly into the stream which flowed into the River. I took a couple pictures of it too. My heart started pounding as I realized I had discovered a major source of contamination that was fouling the River for several miles.

I could see that the hose was connected to a pump. I was on the edge of a construction site; standing in a large undisturbed forested buffer between it and the River. The other end of the hose ran to a hole that had a huge backhoe in the middle of it digging as fast as it could. The backhoe was loading clay into dump trucks. There must have been water in the hole; they were pumping it out as they excavated.

I decided to go back through the woods, get the car, and find whoever was in charge. Since this was happening before my eyes I knew I had to try and put a stop to it. I drove up to the company trailer. That is usually where the foreman or engineer in charge of the project is located. However, no one was there. I found the nearest workman and asked who was in charge. I was dressed in blue jeans, a flannel shirt, and work boots. He asked me if I was looking for a job, because if I was they weren't hiring. I said "No, I'm with the State and I need to speak with whoever is in charge." He pointed to the guy operating the backhoe in the hole. I walked over to get as close to the equipment as I could and started waving to get his attention. Who knows what he thought I was doing; time is money on a construction site like this but he shut down the machine and came over.

I think he was so shocked that I interrupted him, that when I introduced myself and asked him to turn off the pump he did not argue. He explained he had to pump out rainwater that filled up the excavation over the weekend. I told him it was violation of State law to pump clay directly into the brook and that I had been a couple of miles downstream looking at something else when I noticed it and traced it back to him. I got the name of the company, the project owner's, and explained they were liable for fines up to ten thousand dollars.

I went back to the road crossing. I searched the car to see if I had anything to take water samples. I had been in such a hurry to find the source and confront them I forgot until now. One background sample upstream and a couple from downstream would give us a great case. I thought I had a good case anyway, but after the Saco River Case I knew that samples would be important if we had to go to court. However, I discovered the violation by accident. I did not anticipate running into a situation that day that would require sampling equipment. I would have to make do without it.

At this point, I was really excited at my success of discovering a major violation on my own, confronting the violators, and putting a stop to it. I forgot the rest of my itinerary for the day. I went back to the office, told everyone what happened, and wrote up my notes. There was no question that we were going to seek a penalty here.

A week later, I forwarded a letter to the owner of the project and the president of the construction company summarizing my findings. I explained how I was conducting an inspection of unrelated activities, noticed an exceptional amount of siltation in the Nonesuch River, and decided to locate the source. I was able to trace it to a discharge from their project.

The discharge of heavily silted water into a tributary of the River was in itself a violation of State law. In addition, the project had a site development permit issued by the Department. The standard conditions of the permit were violated by not complying with all applicable State laws during construction.

In December, I forwarded a consent agreement assessing an eight thousand dollar penalty. Since I was two miles downstream and noted the contamination, I initially thought to ask for ten thousand dollars, but upon reflection, I could not quite justify it. I gave them credit for being cooperative by immediately shutting down the pump. They also did not have any previous violations.

The project owner said he would agree to whatever we worked out with the contractor. I received a response from the contractor's attorney. Needless to say, he felt the fine was too high. First, I explained why it was not higher. Then I gave him a number of reasons while eight thousand dollars was appropriate: It was a permitted project so they were familiar with the laws. They did not necessarily have to pump the water directly into the stream, it could have been directed to another section of the property where it would not flow into the River. In addition, according to the Department of Marine Resources, a discharge like that had the potential to adversely affect juvenile American Shad and Alewives which were known to be in the Nonesuch River until the middle of November of each year.

We went back and forth on the penalty amount. No remediation was necessary; once the pump was shut off the source of contamination was stopped. I drove out to the crossing the day following my initial discovery and noted the River was running clear again. Their initial position was to receive a warning and no penalty. Since they didn't have any prior violations they did not want their name besmirched with adverse publicity. I responded this was not acceptable, but I would lower the penalty to seventy five hundred dollars.

The attorney countered with fifteen hundred dollars and raised the issue of the lack of water samples. Although I did not acknowledge it directly to him, it was a weakness in the case, so I responded with an offer of five thousand dollars. He countered with two thousand dollars. It was now April. I was running out of patience so I threatened him with filing a complaint in court. He said let's go.

The Deputy Attorney General who handled the Saco River Case also took this one. Sometimes all it takes to reach an agreement are new faces at the table. Since I felt I had reached an impasse with the defendant's attorney he took over the lead for the negotiations. In May, he talked them into accepting a four thousand dollar penalty. Not as much as I would have preferred, but a whole lot more than the nothing that was their initial negotiating stance.

We were pleased with the resolution of the case. It was a good example of the Department taking a proactive approach to detecting and resolving violations of State law. While I personally would have preferred a higher penalty it was still a good settlement. However, I had other tools at my disposal to still utilize.

Over the years, reporters periodically interviewed me concerning cases they wrote stories about. The day after the Board approved the agreement, I called a reporter with the Portland Press Herald I had discussed other cases with. I told him about the violation, why it was a problem, how I found it, and the terms of the settlement. I even compared it to the Saco River Case. I made sure he had the proper spelling of the name of the contractor. The call resulted in a nice ten inch column describing the entire incident and resolution. It was great publicity for the Department's efforts and put other developers and permit holders on notice to comply with the law.

TRIBUTARY OF LONG CREEK II

In early March, I received an anonymous complaint that someone was placing fill in a brook at the intersection of County Road and Spring Street in Westbrook.

I was somewhat familiar with the general area which contained several light industrial parks. When I reached the site I discovered it appeared to be yet another commercial subdivision under construction. There was a sign advertising lots for sale. I think the land closest to the road was formerly farm land. The access road had been completed and three lots were stripped and graded.

The ground was still partially covered with snow. However, most of it was melting and the lots were all mud because there was no vegetation. A small brook ran through the site. The water was brown from all the eroding soils. As I approached for a closer look, my boots became covered with sticky mud. I followed the brook downstream to an adjacent parcel of land and saw that it flowed into a larger stream. A review of a map indicated that the brook was a tributary of Long Creek which in turn was a tributary of the Fore River.

I also went upstream to locate the source of the brook. Just across the property boundary was a small pond that was approximately forty feet across. It looked very deep and must have been spring fed. Cattails lined the bank where the water was shallower. I took a water sample at the mouth of the pond which was the headwater of the brook. It was ice cold, clear, and looked good enough to drink. This was to be my background sample. Its analysis would tell us the condition of the water before it flowed through the construction site. See Figure 10.

I walked downstream and took another water sample from the brook just beyond the property line. A comparison of the two samples would reveal what effect the construction activities had on the brook's water as it flowed through the site. To complete my documentation of the site I took some pictures and made note of my sampling points. I also noted the lack of erosion controls and the general condition of the site.

Upon returning to the office I asked a colleague from the Water Division to help me analyze the samples. By analyzing a known volume of water you can calculate the amount of solids (level of turbidity) in it. We strained equal amounts of water from each sample through extremely fine porous ceramic filters.

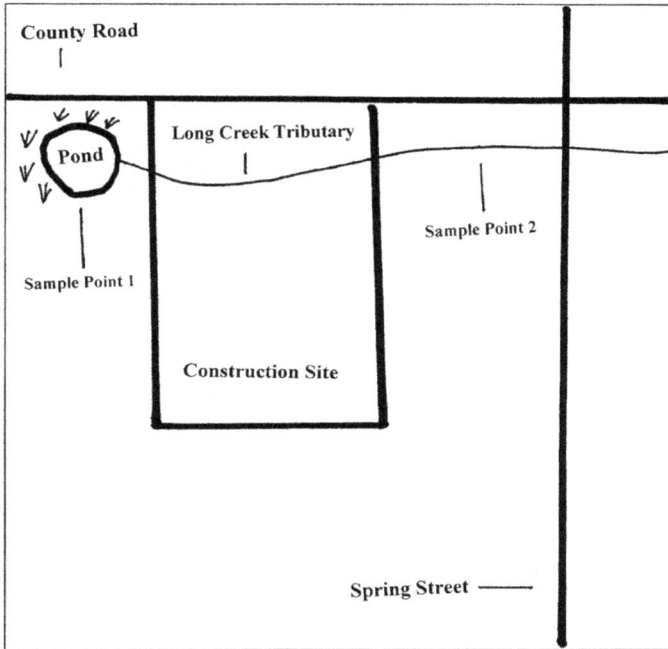

Figure 10 – Tributary of Long Creek – Westbrook

Prior to straining the sample, the filters were washed, cleaned with acid, dried and weighed. After straining the samples through their respective filters they are dried overnight in a desiccator to eliminate any moisture. The filters are then weighed again. The additional weight of each filter is from the suspended material in the water.

By analyzing upstream and downstream samples you get a clear picture of what the water is naturally loaded with and then what it picks up as a result of the erosion from the construction activities. The "clean" background sample contained four and a half milligrams of suspended solids per liter. The "dirty" downstream sample contained three hundred eighty milligrams of solids per liter. The project's activities resulted in an eighty five hundred percent increase in the load of suspended solids in to the brook.

We had a solid case in a rapidly developing commercial area so we decided to pursue a consent agreement.

I was able to identify the project owner from the information on the sign at the development's entrance. A check of our records indicated they had obtained a site development permit. A review of the permit revealed they violated conditions of the permit since the erosion control plan was not followed which resulted in the siltation of the brook. In addition, the siltation was also an illegal discharge into waters of the State.

I contacted the company and explained I had been out to the project site. I expressed concern about the condition of the brook which was a direct result of a violation of their permit. I requested they get out there as soon as possible to erect temporary erosion controls. I also took the opportunity to inform them of the impending enforcement action. We agreed to meet on site the following week. When I arrived the company representative had a crew at work installing erosion control materials. They seemed to be cooperative, but only sprung into action when I came back to the site.

In May, I forwarded a consent agreement that assessed a six thousand dollar penalty. They signed and returned it without comment. That was the first and last time that ever happened. I thought, maybe I should have asked for a higher penalty.

I believe this case was resolved so quickly due to the experience I gained handling the Saco and Nonesuch River cases. With these earlier violations, I was learning as I went along what the important aspects of the cases were. By the third time around I knew how to put it all together to present a strong enforcement action. My documentation of the violation, especially the water samples, left little room for the defendant to maneuver.

TRIBUTARY OF LONG CREEK III

In late March, I had scheduled time to conduct a follow-up inspection of the erosion controls at the subdivision in the previous case.

It had rained heavily the day before. The sky was slate gray with a slight drizzle still falling. While traveling on Spring Street, near the Westbrook/South Portland town line, I noticed an unusual amount of turbidity in what I thought might be another tributary of Long Creek. I started to have flashbacks of my experience with the Nonesuch River.

I parked the car on the shoulder of the road near the stream crossing. The stream was swollen from all the rain. It spilled on to its floodplain with the muddy water flowing through clumps of high brown grass. I grabbed my camera and some sample bags (I always carried some with me now) and headed upstream.

Trying to go in a straight line along the stream and keeping dry was not easy with all the thick undergrowth on the shoreline. It turned out I didn't have far to go to find what I was looking for. After walking about a hundred yards, the woods opened up to a clearing. Directly in my path was a large earthen berm about twenty feet high. I was at one corner; it extended at least a hundred feet to my left and right. In either direction were drainage ditches that ran along its base. I was standing at their confluence; where they formed the stream I noticed from the road. The berm and all the soil adjacent to the ditches had been graded and left exposed with no form of erosion controls. With the ground thawing and the spring rains falling, the erosion of these loose soils had begun.

I jumped across the ditch, which was only four feet wide, and sunk up to my ankles in mud. I climbed up the berm. At the top, I discovered that the berm was actually the sides of a manmade pond. It looked as if the pond was positioned right in the middle of a former stream. The pond was lined with heavy plastic. It appeared to be the type of plastic used to line landfills to keep leachate from seeping into the groundwater. The pond was half full with rain water.

Although I had never been there before, I suspected I stumbled onto the site of the municipal landfill that served the greater

Portland area. I figured it was some type of collection pond as I could see an adjacent area that had been cleared, leveled, and divided by low dikes. These were probably new "cells" for the landfill that would soon receive ash from the new incinerator they were constructing. (This was a separate project from the one discussed in the Saco River Case.) I knew that a permit must have been issued to authorize this work. The question was "were they following it?" It appeared, at the least, their construction activities caused a discharge of silt into State waters.

I walked around to the left side of the pond. I found that the water in this ditch originated from runoff between the new cells and the berm. While it was flowing fairly fast, it was only a couple of inches deep and would most likely dry up when the rain stopped. The water was muddy at its sources and; therefore, would not make a good background sample. Walking over to the right branch, I followed it upstream to its sources. It disappeared into an adjacent grass covered field. Even though it did not have a mineral bottom, it was a defined channel that was the source of this branch. It ran clear with long grasses pointing their way downstream. I was able to get a clean background sample. I then went down below the confluence, at the point where there was one defined channel, and took another sample. The samples were taken well above and well below the disturbed areas so the difference between them would provide a good illustration of the impacts of their activities. See Figure 11.

Upon returning to the car, I made notes of my observations and recorded the sampling points. When I got back to the office I located their permits. A solid waste permit was issued to expand the landfill and a stream alteration permit was issued for the construction of the leachate collection pond. They had obtained permission to redefine the channel during construction. There were also provisions for erosion controls which were not in evidence during my inspection.

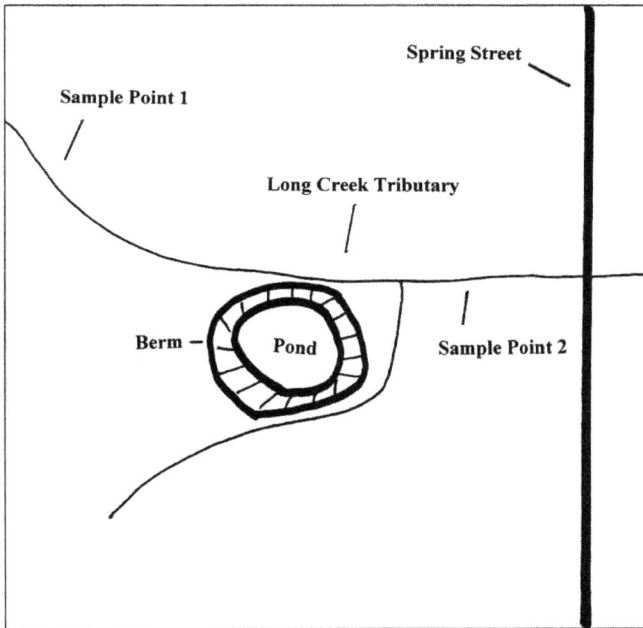

Figure 11 — Tributary of Long Creek — South Portland

Analysis of the background sample indicated the water "normally" contained three milligrams per liter of suspended solids. Analysis of the "dirty" sample indicated it contained two hundred sixty milligrams per liter. Their activities resulted in an eighty six hundred percent increase in suspended solids in the stream's water.

This case was a natural for a consent agreement. As with the previous case, they violated their permits and State discharge laws. In addition, we had the responsibility to be consistent in the manner we handled similar violations. Since we had initiated an action with the developer of the nearby project for their impacts to Long Creek it was our obligation to do the same here.

The facility was owned and operated by a quasi-municipal corporation that managed solid waste disposal on behalf of its twenty member municipalities in Cumberland and York Counties. I contacted the corporate officer in charge of their operations and informed him of my inspection and the violations. We made an appointment to meet at the site the next day.

The operator also invited his contractor to meet with us. It turned out the company that conducted the work was the same one responsible for the Bennet Road strip mine violation. This guy was just a foreman so I didn't bother to discuss the violation and enforcement action with him. I actually had previously scheduled a meeting, for the next day, with officers of his company to discuss the final details of the consent agreement for the strip mine. I figured I would raise this case with them at that time. Meanwhile, we went over the facility operator's permit and their responsibility for erosion controls.

Upon concluding our discussion about the pond, the operator took me on a tour of his facility. There were two huge pyramids, at least one hundred feet high, that were constructed from the trash that had been dumped over the last decade. They were on the third one which was going to have to be closed soon too. They were seeking permission to allow them to place more trash on one of the other mounds until the new incinerator and the cells were operational.

The site was selected for a landfill due to its geology. As it turned out, under the topsoil, was a deposit of marine clay that the operator maintained was several hundred feet thick. Clay is very impermeable and water tends to run off it. This makes for an excellent dump site because the leachate will not be able to seep into the groundwater. However, the problem you are left with, which is more manageable, is controlling surface water contamination. They would address this by diverting the surface drainage to the leachate collection pond. From there it was discharged into the local sewer system for treatment.

The next day the company officers for the contractor came to my office. I held the meeting in a colleague's office. It was very small with an oversized desk in it. I was only expecting two people to show up but four came. There was barely enough room for all of them to fit in the office. I had them sitting shoulder to shoulder right in front of the desk. We discussed the strip mine and came to terms on the agreement. Then I told them of my discovery earlier in the week, how it was a violation, and that enforcement action would be taken there too. This was almost surreal. All four of these men were twice my age and had been in the construction business for an average of twenty years and here I was lecturing them like a school principal on how they screwed up again. They did not say much in response. I think they were stunned by the whole thing.

In April, I went out to the site and confirmed that erosion controls had been put in place. In July, I stopped by again and all the exposed soils had been stabilized with grass.

The only thing left to do was to reach agreement on a penalty. Due to my workload, I was not able to forward a consent agreement until the Fall. They thought the seven thousand five hundred dollars I proposed was too high. I pointed out the settlement for six thousand dollars we reached on the project nearby, for a similar violation. In addition, I said I also weighed the contractor's previous violation which was also a violation of the site development law. They signed.

I felt good about this settlement because I had discovered the violation and took action to correct the resultant problems. My growing skill as an investigator enabled me to develop a really strong case. Another measure of success was knowing that I had been able to mitigate some of the intense development pressure that the Long Creek watershed was being subjected to.

AFTERWORD

Environmental laws are intended to protect water, air, and land resources for the common good. Water is a public – and exhaustible – resource that the government has an obligation to manage wisely. Toxic air emissions are not confined by property or political boundaries. Development and industrial activities often have impacts beyond their property boundaries as well. When the government sets standards to protect the environment, it generally attempts to strike a balance between mitigating the impacts of activities by individuals for profit with the preservation of natural resources.

Government has several policy tools that can be utilized to protect the environment. Typical strategies are to regulate activities in ecologically sensitive areas and to control emissions of pollutants. Once the policy selection is made, no matter what the law or standards that the government decides are best for the public good, protection of the environment will always rely on a credible enforcement presence that provides an incentive for the regulated community to comply. If no one is out there checking, corporate self-interest will generally lead to short cuts to maximize profits at the expense of the common will. An overarching goal of enforcement action is the fair treatment of businesses and individuals in order to maintain a level economic playing field to prevent those breaking the law from realizing an advantage over those who comply.

The routine inspection efforts that comprise the job of protecting the environment should focus on problem facilities or those which present higher risks to surrounding communities and ecosystems. Inspection efforts also serve to screen violations and ensure the application of limited resources for the resolution of the most egregious ones. Thoughtfulness and selectivity are important due to the large amount of time and effort that goes into any one case.

Enforcement action is typically taken when there is strong evidence to prove the violation and/or the violators are caught in the act. Also, situations that involve circumstances where the opportunity exists for additional environmental damage to occur will result in action. Action for permit violations should be paramount as well because there is a need to demonstrate that following it is as important as obtaining it. This is a point that needs to be emphasized in the climate change debate when "cap and trade" is highlighted by some as the regulatory solution of choice to reduce air pollution. The latter term refers to trading permits that allow facilities to pollute. From an implementation standpoint, a straightforward alternative to creating a new permit system and related bureaucracy would be to modify the existing tax code to assess a carbon tax on fossil fuels.

In summary, the ultimate goal of any enforcement program, whether to protect the environment or prevent financial wrongdoing, is to influence human behavior to keep activity within acceptable boundaries delineated by government policies. Therefore, those programs with a strong verification and compliance framework, and that provide technical assistance to build compliance capacity are the ones that succeed. Voluntary pledges and weak verification systems, generally don't. As Ronald Reagan once said in a different context, insist that we "trust, but verify."

SELECT BIBLIOGRAPHY

Alden, Peter. *National Audubon Society Field Guide to New England,* 8th *Edition.* Chanticleer Press, Inc. New York. 2007.

Amos, William, and Stephen Amos. *Atlantic and Gulf Coasts.* Alfred A. Knopf, New York. 1985.

Hoffman, Jennifer. *Ocean Science.* Hydra Publishing, Irvington, NY. 2007.

Kelly, Joseph T., and Alice R. Kelley, and Orrin Pilkey, Sr. *Living with the Coast of Maine.* Duke University Press. Durham. 1989.

Lambert, David. *The Field Guide to Geology, New Edition.* Checkmark Books, NY. 2007.

Maley, Terry S. *Field Geology Illustrated, Second Edition.* Sheridan Books, Ann Arbor. 2005.

McMenamin, Mark A.S. *Geology.* Hydra Publishing, Irvington, NY. 2007.

Niering, William, A. *Wetlands,* Alfred A. Knopf, New York, 1987.

Stine, Jeffrey K. *America's Forested Wetlands: From Wasteland to Valuable Resource.* Forest History Society. Durham. 2008.

Tiner, Ralph W. *In Search of Swampland: A Wetland Sourcebook and Field Guide*, Second Edition. Rutgers University Press, New Brunswick, NJ. 2005.

WEBSITES

MAINE DEPARTMENT OF ENVIRONMENTAL PROTECTION: www.maine.gov/dep/

SMITHSONIAN INSTITUTION: www.si.edu

UNITED STATES ENVIRONMENTAL PROTECTION AGENCY: www.epa.gov

ACKNOWLEDGMENTS

I want to thank the following individuals for making this book possible:

Don Kale for putting me in the field.

Steve Pelletier for giving me the original idea to write from this perspective.

Bella Pagano for her work on the illustrations and Rose Grandfield for her contributions to the cover design.

NOTES

[1] Stegner, Wallace, *Where the Bluebird Sings to the Lemonade Springs.* (Penguin Books, New York 1992),132.

[2] Duhigg, Charles, *Clean Water Laws Are Neglected, at a Cost in Suffering,* The New York Times, NY, September 13, 2009.

[3] In addition to my direct supervisor, who I had daily contact with at the office, we also had a chain of command at the headquarters in the state capitol. In ascending order of responsibility this included a Bureau Director, Deputy Commissioner, Commissioner, and the Board of Environmental Protection (Board). Appointed by the Governor, the Commissioner was essentially the Chief Executive Officer of the Department. The Board is composed of ten volunteer citizen members who are appointed by the Governor and confirmed by the Legislature for staggered 4-year terms.

The Board is charged by statute with providing "informed, independent and timely decisions on the interpretation, administration and enforcement of the laws relating to environmental protection and to provide for credible, fair and responsible public participation in department decisions." [38 M.R.S.A. section 341-B]. The Board accomplishes its statutory charge through: rulemaking, licensing decisions on selected permit applications, reviewing the Commissioner's licensing and enforcement actions, and recommending changes in the law to the Legislature. While the Board is part of the Department of Environmental Protection, the Board has decision-making authority independent of the Commissioner.

[4] During my tenure in Maine, statutory authority specified a penalty range of between $100 - $10,000 per day per violation. For example, for an illegal discharge that took place during the course of one day, the maximum penalty could be $10,000, or an illegal structure built without permits and in existence for one year could, theoretically be assessed a minimum penalty of $36,500 (365x$100).

[5] Some regulatory organizations use very detailed policies that attempt to anticipate every violation and even describe extenuating circumstances that lead to penalty reductions. The base penalty is often determined by considering two factors: the potential to harm human health and the environment and the extent of deviation from a statutory or regulatory requirement. Many civil penalty statutes include specific criteria that the regulatory agency considers when assessing a penalty. The number and content of the criteria in statutes are diverse and generally range between as few as three, or as many as ten. The criteria generally fall into ten broad categories: 1. economic benefit from delayed compliance; 2. the gravity (seriousness) of the violation; 3. the degree of the violators culpability; 4. the extent of the violator's good faith efforts to comply (or lack thereof); 5. the history of prior violations; 6. the economic impact of a penalty on the violator (ability to pay); 7. the deterrent effect of the penalty; 8. the cost to the agency of enforcing against the violator or of cleaning up its pollution; 9. a balancing of the competing interests served by penalizing or not penalizing the violator; and 10. other relevant factors.

⁶ These rules apply to proceedings in Maine District Court involving alleged violations of land use laws and ordinances, whether administered and enforced primarily at the state or the local level as set forth in 4 M.R.S.A. § 152(6). Certification standards and a program to certify familiarity with the court for Department of Environmental Protection employees is set forth in Title 38, section 342, subsection 7.

⁷ Of the eighty miles of sand beaches in Maine, the majority of the original dune fields have been heavily altered or developed. The beaches with large undeveloped dune fields remaining are typically public lands found in state parks.

⁸ The board of selectmen is commonly the executive arm of the government of New England towns. The function of the board of selectmen differs from state to state, and can differ within a given state depending on the type of governance under which a town operates. Selectman is almost always a part-time position that pays only a token salary. The basic function consists of calling town meetings, calling elections, appointing employees, setting certain fees, overseeing certain volunteer and appointed bodies, and creating basic regulations.

INDEX

INDEX

citation, 58
clam, 41
clay, 134
Clean Water Act, 45
climate change, vii, 42, 138
coastal wetland, 36, 39, 40, 42,
    48, 51, 53, 55, 56, 59, 61,
    62, 65, 68
coastal zone, 42
code enforcement officer (CEO),
    51, 52, 54, 55, 59, 62, 77
coffer dam, 114
Commissioner, 11, 78, 82, 87,
    94-96
complaints, 5, 8, 10, 17, 32,
    59, 105, 107, 113
compliance, viii, 2- 4, 6, 8, 10,
    47, 51, 78-80, 82-85, 88,
    92, 113, 116, 138
consent agreement, 6, 8, 11,
    21-23, 25, 57, 60, 61, 75,
    78-80, 84-86, 92, 118,
    125, 130, 133-135
continuance, 60, 62
corporate self-interest, 137
crabs, 41
Cumberland County, 73, 90

dam, 16, 32, 33, 36-38, 114,
    117-119
Dayton, 106
defendant, 7-9, 11, 20, 60, 85,
    93-95, 127, 130

Department of Agriculture
    (DOA), 106, 108, 109, 111
deterrence, 2, 3, 8, 9
dike, 52-56, 61
dilution, 28
District Court, 58, 60
dogwood, 28
dredge, 30, 37, 38, 42, 44, 56
drinking water, 99
ducks, 40, 56
dune, 65-68
due process, 58
ecosystem, 14, 19

Eliot, 51, 76, 77, 80
emergent plants, 27
enforcement, 1, 2, 138
enforcement action(s), 1, 3,
    4, 24, 36, 37, 46, 47, 50,
    54, 55, 74, 103, 117, 130,
    134, 137
enforcement discretion, viii, 8
erosion, 14, 16, 17, 21, 23,
    30, 37, 40, 65-69, 71, 79,
    128-135
eutrophication, 30
evidence, 5, 6, 8, 9, 57-60, 76, 88,
    108, 120-122, 132, 138
explosives, 31, 32

fieldwork, vii
filter feeders, 14
fines, 1, 81, 125

148

ABOUT THE AUTHOR

Peter Pagano is an advisor to the natural science research units of the Smithsonian Institution. He worked in a field office for the Maine Department of Environmental Protection for several years. For fifteen years, he was an advisor to the senior management and political leaders of the United States Environmental Protection Agency. As a Brookings Institution Fellow during the 105th Congress, he was an environmental policy advisor to a United States Senator. He received an undergraduate degree in Environmental Science from Colby College and a graduate degree in Public Policy from the University of Southern Maine.

www.ingramcontent.com/pod-product-compliance
Lightning Source LLC
Chambersburg PA
CBHW050127280326
41933CB00010B/1283

* 9 7 8 0 6 1 5 3 4 3 5 2 5 *